Pra

JUMPING FRO

M000202710

**GOLD WINNER, 2019 IBPA Benjamin Franklin Award,
Best New Voice: Nonfiction**

"Reading this book gives one the opportunity to go inside a soldier's mind, living his real-life experience that most people could never imagine. Obviously, a special father-daughter relationship exists for John and Lori to have taken the time, given the effort, and endured the emotional toll that it took to write this book. I applaud them both for their personal commitment to share John's story. Americans need to know what the Vietnam War was really like so that our country doesn't repeat the mistakes of the past—as well as recognize and show more appreciation for the personal sacrifices our soldiers have made for all of us."

—PAUL MEANS, brother of late soldier, Ronnie Means,
who served with John in the 101st Airborne

"From her dad's childhood and Army training prior to going overseas to the jungles and battlefields of Vietnam, John Stillman's daughter Lori takes the reader on an accurate, humorous, and at times harrowing journey. Vietnam-era veterans will identify with joining the service or getting drafted, as well as with the life-changing experience of going from civilian to soldier and back again, while civilians and non-combat veterans will have a new understanding and respect for what our brave warriors experienced in the early days of the Vietnam war. From start to finish, the authors have crafted a page-turning memoir, one that Lori clearly wrote as a heartfelt tribute with deep love and respect for her father."

—ALLAN KUHLMAN, Army veteran, 101st Airborne

"*Jumping from Helicopters* grabbed me on the first page and I couldn't put it down. It was like reading my own story through John's words, having served with him in Vietnam, in the same platoon and company. . . . From An Lo village on the Song Bo River to the Ashau Valley deep in the mountains, I could feel the heat and smell the dirt. . . . Like John, I was home a long time before I really came home. Kudos to Lori for gently pulling out the deeply buried memories, and for helping her dad to tell his story."

—SSG WAYNE DUGGER,
101st Airborne, 1st of 502nd, B company

"Being a current-day veteran myself, I can say that not many civilians—especially today's teens—have any idea what soldiers like John Stillman went through to defend freedom in a foreign land during the Vietnam War. *Jumping from Helicopters*, from its intense moments of chaos and horror to its welcome injections of humor, paints that picture vividly and serves as a true eye-opener."

—CARL ORLANDO,
Spec/E4, 2nd ID–101st ABN 86–89, Army 04–10 ANG

"John Stillman's account of his experience in Vietnam is simultaneously brutal, heartbreaking, and tender. It's painful to see him being rewired in real time, all the while knowing now the long-term impact of those experiences. At the heart of the book is the relationship between John and his family, especially evident with his daughter, Lori. This is a must-read for anyone wishing to understand the cost of war and the commitment to country."

—AMY SHAW,
Senior Vice President of Engagement and Content,
Nine Network of Public Media

JUMPING FROM

FROM

HELICOPTERS

JUMPING FROM HELICOPTERS

A VIETNAM MEMOIR

JOHN STILLMAN
WITH
LORI STILLMAN

TURTLE CREEK

Turtle Creek Publishing
PO Box 173
Richwoods, MO 63071
turtlecreekpublishing@outlook.com

Published 2018

ISBN: 978-1-7327361-3-9 pb
ISBN: 978-1-7327361-2-2 hc
ISBN: 978-1-7327361-1-5 ebk

Library of Congress Control Number: 2018910347

Editing and book design by Stacey Aaronson

Printed in the United States of America

To the 58,000 plus names on the Vietnam Memorial Wall,
they are the true heroes of the war. They gave all.

This book is an authentic depiction of the conditions of US soldiers fighting in the Vietnam War. As such, certain words are used that some may find offensive; however, the authors wish to convey that in the case of what are today considered derogatory terms, all uses of such terms are in reference to "the enemy" during wartime, not in referring to the Vietnamese as a whole. These words, similar to others that at one time were not initially used as derogatory but became so over time, are merely a reflection of the accuracy of the time and circumstance, not of the authors' current vernacular or viewpoints.

INTRODUCTION

I remember the first time I saw the tattoo. I was just shy of five years old, and my dad was sitting at the dinner table telling Mom about his workday. Like every other day, he had gone to work wearing a long-sleeve shirt, but on that steamy hot day, he had changed into a cool white tee when he got home. The look was so foreign to me that it was the equivalent of seeing Mister Rogers without a sweater.

As he reached to scratch an itch, the already short sleeve slid upward and a flash of color on his bicep caught my eye. Wanting to see more, I inched closer and carefully lifted his sleeve to peek under it. Possibly hoping I'd be satisfied just by seeing it, he continued chatting with my mom. But my curious mind wasn't satisfied in the least. At the first break in their conversation, I exploded with questions.

"Daddy, how did you get that color on your skin? Will it wash off? What are those pictures of?"

Patiently, he explained the tattoo process—adding that it was extremely painful as an extra deterrent—pointing to each image: boots with wings, a parachute, his name. He said it showed that he jumped from planes and helicopters but that he didn't think much about it anymore.

I was left with the thought that he must have been forced to get it, because why else would he hide it? But that was the end of our conversation about it.

It wasn't until high school that I read a paragraph on the

Vietnam conflict in my history class. It wasn't much, but it was more than my father had told me. With my curiosity piqued, I remembered being around twelve when my parents had invited friends over to view some slides, and that no kids were allowed in the room. Wondering if the slides were of the war, I came home and dug out the off-limits box from under the stairs. Holding up slide after slide to the light, I finally found what I was looking for: evidence that my father had fought in the war. It was then that I realized he had done more than jump from choppers; he had killed people too. Images of dead people, lying in tall grasses, brought tears to my eyes. I didn't dare ask Dad more, though. Something told me he wouldn't want to talk about it.

In my thirties, I fell hard in love with a military man. He gave me his dog tags and a deployment coin to hold on to as he left for yet another stint overseas. But though he physically came home afterward, the man I loved didn't. He ended our wild love affair with a few sentences about how he had changed, and how he was sorry he didn't feel the same, but that he just didn't feel anything.

I knew as much about his war as I did about my father's. In my heartbroken state, I made a decision to find out more—how the military are trained to kill, what happens to them after they've been immersed in this level of violence, and how I could help someone diagnosed with PTSD, post-traumatic stress disorder. With my lost love on my mind, my focus was on the currently deployed military. What I didn't realize was that they weren't the only ones struggling to cope with having been in a battle zone. My own father had been struggling privately for years.

Shortly after my breakup in 2012, my father was invited to a Veteran's Day celebration at his high school. He thought he would attend and merely be acknowledged, but once there, the men were asked if they would talk to students in classrooms and share some of their experience in Vietnam. Caught off guard, my father wanted to slip out quietly, but he was sitting in the back of the room where he couldn't leave without being obvious. So, not wanting to embarrass himself, he reluctantly agreed.

The next day, we got together and he told me that after speaking to the first class, they asked him to address another . . . and another. By the third, it became a little easier for him, and when the bell rang, no one wanted to leave.

Feeling as if a door had been opened, I gingerly asked him, "So what was it like for you to fight in the war?"

He looked away for a moment, seeming torn about how much to say to me. Finally, he merely said, "I was home a long time before I was actually home."

I don't know if it was my broken heart he was trying to help heal, but those words were enough to shift my focus toward a bigger project.

A week or so later, I sat down again with my father. Taking his hand, I said, "You know I want to write a book, right?"

I was pretty sure I'd never actually mentioned that to him, but he answered yes all the same.

"Would you like to tell your story?" I asked.

Emotionless, and without so much as a facial gesture, he replied, "Sure."

Looking back, it was odd that I would ask him to embark on such a deep excavation of memories he had barely begun to acknowledge openly. Just a few years before, we had stumbled across the traveling Vietnam memorial wall and I wanted to stop and see it. As we walked along it, observing the thousands of names, I asked him if he knew anyone.

"Nope, no one," was his response.

In my naïveté, I said, "Wow, how lucky are you to not know anyone listed here."

I now know he had lied.

In January of 2013, my father and I sat down to begin talking about his time in Vietnam. I expected all he would have were his memories, which might have been spotty after all these years, but there was more. Dad had not only kept a journal while in Vietnam, but he had written letters from overseas to my mom—who at that time was his girlfriend—and she had kept all of them. We were also able to obtain the daily report from the department of defense that charted his whereabouts and activity during the months he was there.

With all of these documents at my disposal—most of which hadn't been read for decades—I imagined I would be able to piece together my father's time in Vietnam and paint a decent picture in words of that chapter of his life. What I didn't realize was that while the journal, the letters, and the reports would play significant roles in our journey together, all of it would be nothing compared to his memory . . .

PROPERTY OF
THE ARMY

I WAS EIGHT YEARS OLD. The old maple trees lined the street, making it shaded even during high noon. I marched along in the midwest humidity, sweat beading on my face, then paused to wipe the moisture as I admired the neighbor's new '56 Buick. It was my favorite color: bright red.

I bent over to roll up my uniform pants for the third time, then used my spit to polish my boot and remove a scuff of mud. That's when I caught my reflection in the waxed car and couldn't help but smile. I looked so distinguished. The men on TV, the ones who marched stiff-legged with one arm swinging, they were the ones I mimicked. I fantasized that the uniform I was wearing came from one of those guys, but I didn't know for sure because it was a gift to me. My dad's friend at the American Legion somehow got hold of a genuine Nazi uniform and thought I'd like it. It was missing the helmet, but that didn't stop me. I dug around the kitchen and found that Mom's mixing bowl made a great substitution. I cradled my wooden rifle in my left arm and marched swinging the other.

I smiled as I remembered Mom shouting out the screen

door to get back in the house immediately. I had no idea at the time why she was so panicked. Now it's clear to me: I had been imitating those Nazis for the whole neighborhood to see. As I took off running toward the house, the too-long pants unrolled and sent me crashing to the ground. The mixing bowl tumbled down the sidewalk, and blood soaked into the fabric of the pants from my skinned-up knees.

"What's so funny?" Sergeant Ruper asked.

Startled from my reverie, I realized I had laughed out loud.

"Nothing," I said, "only Nazi stories."

He started to say something and then must have changed his mind.

I scanned the interior of the helicopter as the repetitive thump and whoosh of the chopper's Huey blades filled the air. I was coated with sweat and the youthful anticipation of being the company's first chopper ride in-country. Positioned in the middle, I glanced around at the boots of the other men, feeling eager in my fresh green uniform, and instinctively reached down to wipe the dust from mine. Some things will never change; my boots needed to be clean.

Sergeant Ruper, the squad leader, sat next to me. He was born and raised in New Jersey, and that northeastern accent was evident when he talked. Sometimes it was so thick that I had trouble making out what he said.

This was Ruper's second time in Vietnam—his first was with the 173rd Airborne, and this time he was with the 101st. During that chopper ride, my eyes fixed on his CIB—combat infantry badge—and jump wings on his uniform and felt a degree of safety with him; after all, he had volunteered to come back to Vietnam, so it couldn't be that bad. He knew what he was doing, and I wanted to soak up everything. He gave me a ride from Fort Campbell, Kentucky, to Fort Gordon, Georgia, to pick up my car, and the 444-mile trip helped me to get to know him. I had the utmost respect for the guy.

Ruper felt like a father to the whole squad. At the ripe-old age of nearly twenty-six, he treated each guy like a son, always talking to them on their level. Because he was full of experience, especially in combat, I looked to him for advice, to know the correct move. I was sure I was going to be like him.

A rush of air filled the helicopter and felt chilled compared to the ground temperature. The moisture that had formed in beads on my face dried as I cooled off. Choppers flew parallel to us on each side, carrying the best soldiers. Sergeant said something to me, but I couldn't hear him over the thumps.

The mood in the chopper was upbeat, especially from Ronnie Means. His green eyes disappeared into small slits as his whole face smiled. Means was a stocky farm boy from Cherokee, Iowa, who looked like he should have been uncomfortable in the chopper with his comrades only inches away. With his broad shoulders, he had to twist his upper body to have some space—but if he was uncomfortable, his face didn't show it. Instead, he looked giddy.

The summer before Means joined the Army, he took a job building concrete silos. He wasn't only after the pay but the hard, manual labor to help get him fit for his military career. He had a plan to chase high rank after graduating top of his class at Fort Benning. He wanted to be the best of the best, and I didn't have any doubt he'd achieve it.

I didn't hit it off with Means until we spent five hours together on a bus. Though we had trained together for months, and slept in bunks separated by one, there hadn't been too many conversations. But road trips brought out my talkative side, and on our last visit home before going to Vietnam, we passed the hours from St. Louis, Missouri, to Fort Campbell, Kentucky, getting to know each other.

On that dark bus, we talked about our younger brothers who were close to the same age, and about our sisters we teased every chance we got. Means laughed when I told him how I played a Nazi in the streets, then he shared stories of playing with his little green army men, his favorite toys growing up. It was during that trip that we discovered we had both shared the goal of wanting to be in the Army.

As the chopper descended into the tall jungle grass beneath, Means gave me a thumbs up.

"Everyone get out!" Ruper yelled over the slowing helicopter blade.

The guys were all excited, but we moved slowly because of the weight of the gear on our backs. It made the unloading process slow and the sergeant antsy. He kept waving his arm faster and faster over his head. "Move! Move! Move!" Sergeant Ruper's nostrils flared as he motioned for us to head over to a line of trees. As the choppers lifted to pick up more soldiers, I wondered why there weren't enough choppers to move the whole company. Seemed a little impractical to me.

The other thing on my mind was knowing that Bob Hope was performing back at Củ Chi right at that moment. I wanted to write home and tell my folks that I had seen Mr. Hope, but we got sent out for training in the jungle instead. They told us we hadn't earned seeing Bob Hope yet.

As we gathered, my eyes landed on some of the guys from

the 25th who had arrived before us. At that moment, it hit me hard what "earning" entertainment looked like. Looking first at their boots, I saw that in contrast to my shiny pair, theirs were scuffed and caked with dried-up mud. Those boots appeared to have a thousand miles on them—but the faces of the men who wore them had more. It was one of the first things I noticed in Vietnam: that we were wet behind the ears. Our boots were clean, like our faces, and I didn't think anything could change us. But the truth was, those guys who looked like they had years on us in Vietnam often only had weeks.

I hoisted my rucksack higher up on my back and took off jogging to catch up with the rest of the guys. Everyone had slipped their gear off and sat down so I followed suit. Platoon Sergeant Allen was standing there waiting for us.

Sergeant Allen's face had the texture of leather, scarred from acne and almost flat. His voice was deep and gravelly, and the only time a cigarette wasn't hanging from his mouth was when he was sleeping. He reminded me of my Uncle Bill, who barked and yelled like him. When one of the other sergeants called him Spike, I realized I wasn't the only one to see a bulldog resemblance.

This was his second tour in Vietnam, so he knew it well.

"Men, this would be the Ho Bo Woods," he said. The cigarette stuck to his dry lips and moved up and down with his words. He opened his arms as wide as possible to show the whole area around them. "This is a fucking dense jungle area that'd been a refuge for the goddamn gooks." He nodded upward. "A little bit north of here is the Iron Triangle. That area also provides thick coverage and protection for those bastards. But don't worry, the Twenty-Fifth has informed us that this area is secure. Today you'll practice some in-country training."

Waite, a small-framed insecure guy from Omaha, Nebraska, sat next to me and inched his hand in the air. I grabbed his sleeve and yanked it down. *Geez, Waite, you're not in school,* I thought.

Spike must have seen the movement because he shook his head as he continued to talk.

"There isn't any need to worry. As I said, this area is secure. The Twenty-Fifth has already been out here and done all the hard work. Get your shit together . . . we'll move out soon."

I looked at Waite. He was so thin that his skin appeared stretched over his bones, especially on his face. How he ever made any decisions baffled me; he always wanted reassurance from someone else. I had seen him actually shaking in his boots at jump school. We were waiting for our turn on the thirty-four-foot training tower when I heard whispers behind me. "I'm going to die . . . I'm afraid of heights." I turned to see Waite, his brown eyes round and bulging.

I couldn't contain my laughter. "You're afraid of heights and you're in jump school?"

He just stared.

I half-joked, "Boy, the signup for a leg unit is out the back door. Get to it."

Later, he shared with me how his father was in the 101st during World War II and was part of the Normandy invasion on D-Day. He felt destined and determined to be Airborne, and that I related to, because it was my goal too. When we graduated, his dad came and pinned his blood wings on him.

Looking back, I should have been nicer to him, shown him more respect for following in his father's footsteps. But teasing him was more fun. He made it through tower training only to be here shaking like a leaf in-country, making him an easy target to harass.

The sweat poured down my face from that short jog away from the chopper, and I had to squint and blink as it burned my eyes. It was December of 1967 in Vietnam. I had always known cold and snow this time of year, but here, the air was so thick and muggy that I struggled to take deep breaths. My body wasn't acclimated to the sauna-like weather, and my jungle fatigues were like wearing wet blankets.

My excitement coupled with nerves and suffocating heat didn't lend to patience as I waited for the command to go, until a high-pitched scream from the depths of the jungle made me forget about the sweat. I squinted into the darkness of the vegetation, my heart racing as I prepared myself for what was going to jump out at us. When the second scream punctuated the canopy, I twisted my panicked face toward Ruper.

My expression made him belly laugh for longer than I was comfortable. "That'd be monkeys screaming," he finally said. "You'll get used to it. Get your gear ready."

I did a quick check. Rucksack, eight one-quart canteens, four hand grenades, two smoke grenades, two claymore mines with a clicker, fifty feet of wire, a bandoleer of M60 ammo for the machine gunner, and thirty shells for my M79, which everyone called the "thumper." My Boy Scout training, alongside the training from the Army, had me prepared to lug thirty pounds of gear on my scrawny frame.

I was busy wiping the dirt from my boots when I heard what I thought were monkeys screaming again, only this time a lot closer. When I looked up, Waite, with his rucksack covering his whole backside, was doing a little jig—those high-pitched sounds were coming from him. He frantically slid off his heavy pack as Sergeant Ruper ran to him. Curiosity had me running over too. When I reached him, I saw that Waite was covered in large crawling insects, red yet transparent, scurrying from the top of his head down his neck.

"Get his fatigues off!" Ruper commanded. "Try to brush them off. Don't try to kill them. They're fire ants!"

But kicking into rescue mode, I instinctively started smacking at them, which caused Waite to scream even louder. He fought us as we pulled at his fatigues.

"Don't try to kill them!" Ruper instructed again, louder. "Brush them off!"

After what seemed like minutes of chaos, we flicked away the last tormenter. Waite leaned over, his hands on his knees, his pale body covered in welts.

"I'm going to die," he moaned. His frail body heaved up and down as he tried to catch his breath.

Suddenly, gunfire made me jump. Waite tripped a few times as he pulled on his pants. I quickly grabbed my gear and my M79.

"Those shots are off in the distance," Ruper clarified. "Cool your jets so you're ready for the real thing. That gunfire's nothing to worry over."

Ruper picked up his gear as helicopters circled overhead and the door gunners started firing. The radio crackled that Alpha company was taking fire from the Viet Cong, or VC as we called them. I figured this was part of the training too, since we were in a secure area. But as the message was repeated, I realized I'd better take this training seriously.

Bravo company—my company—radioed back to hold fire. Sergeant Ruper knew from the coordinates given from Alpha company that if Alpha fired, they would fire directly at us.

Kind of a shitty mistake to make in training, I thought. Believing this would never happen for real, I watched Sarge to see what he would do. He dropped to the ground, synchronized with Means on one side, and I followed on the other. My face fell flat into the moist dirt. Rotting vegetation and insects both dead and alive filled my nose, mouth, and eyes.

"Let's move forward!" I heard Ruper say. We inched the slightest bit and more gunfire rang out. My will to protect myself kicked in at that point, shielding me from guessing how real this training was going to get. My heart was pounding in my chest as I gulped for air.

I heard the radio on Means's back say that two men were killed from A company. Still trying to wrap my head around if this was training or real life, I didn't know what to believe.

With the line blurred, I stuck with believing it was training. Excitement pulsed through me as the helicopter brushed the treetops, with the door gunners rapidly firing into the jungle. I wanted to stand up and cheer but knew better, so I muttered the *yeahs!* quietly in my head.

I felt like the gunners were the heroes of the battle, doing a lot more than we ever could. I wondered how I could switch to that job because it seemed safe. But in that split second, as if in slow motion, the green of the chopper exploded into orange. Heat zapped my face as the door gunner fell from the chopper in a ball of flames and the fiery wreckage plummeted to the ground. When it hit, sparks flew and the chopper broke apart like a burned piece of paper. Ashes floated into the sky, holding my gaze until my brain could process what had happened.

I quickly turned to Ruper. "Did the gooks shoot that

chopper? Was that part of the training? Can they shoot a bird from the sky?"

I waited for Ruper to reassure me, to remind us how Vietnam was a cakewalk, an easy way to collect combat pay. I waited for him to tell us this was all practice and no one was killed. But Ruper said nothing. His mouth was open and he didn't blink. He tried to form words but nothing came out. I stared quietly at him as a bug crawled up his neck and across his cheek. He never brushed it away.

My chest tightened as Ruper finally uttered, "I've fucked up. I've fucked up this time."

A lump formed in my throat as I felt a sense of dread wash over me.

ON-THE-JOB
TRAINING

THE CHOPPERS WE HAD come in on quickly returned to get us out of there. Everyone was in a state of confusion. Our proposed "secure" in-country training left A company short three men—two killed in action and one missing.

They transported us to Củ Chi where a memorial was set up for the men who had died. It reminded me of Memorial Day services that the American Legion put on back at home: the boots, helmets, rifles, and dog tags of the deceased laid out as an homage to the brave.

When the service was over, they passed out our newly earned combat infantry badges—or CIBs—which weren't actually badges but pieces of paper. As I held mine in my hand, I realized that I couldn't have cared less about this so-called honor I had once been eagerly awaiting.

It was then that I overheard the company commander giving orders to Lieutenant Hale to take a group from B company out the next day to find the missing soldier, that A company wasn't able to go look for their own man. Riddled with guilt, I quietly hoped I wouldn't be selected.

Overnight, the plans changed. Whether it was because A company decided to go look for their own guy, or the Army changed its mind, Lieutenant Hale was off the hook. He uttered quiet thanks and we all breathed an internal sigh of relief.

By noon, however, our relief turned to shock and anger. We heard the MIA had been found, shot execution style. No one wanted to say out loud how that meant he was alive when we left and the enemy had found him.

At that point, there wasn't any more talk about training, or practice; it was all real from there on out. I was hopeful that I had seen the worst of it as my platoon readied itself to head out.

After humping for hours weighed down with our gear, I was relieved to see a village. It was deserted, which meant a break for us. Sergeant Allen took us around and had us carefully kick in the huts, ensuring that the area was secure. On my turn I tried to visualize the village occupied, wondering what I would do. Would I rip open the makeshift door and shoot? Luckily, I didn't have to find out.

There wasn't much inside the huts—dirt floors, crude kitchen tools. It took me back to my lessons in grade school about the American Indians. I was surprised at how primitive it was here still as Legg worked through the hut with me, checking things out. I met Don Legg at Fort Campbell—the running joke of why a leg was in the Airborne unit. He was born and raised in West Virginia, and I liked him. I think I was drawn to how opposite he was from me. He never took anything seriously, had a wild sense about him, and was always seeking out adventures.

Legg told me how he and a group of soldiers stole a Volkswagen Beetle to drive back to the Fort from a party night in Nashville one weekend. They hid it in the woods and were cocky about getting away with it. The following weekend, they went to check on it and it was still there, so they piled in and took it to Nashville. They left it in the woods again before they departed for Vietnam. I heard the guys joke about if it would be there when they got home.

Legg was always happy-go-lucky, and that made him a blast to be around. Even if he was in trouble, he didn't seem to care. His attitude searching those huts in the jungle was the same.

After we left the farm village, it wasn't long before we came across some rice paddies. Walking through them proved more challenging than the thick jungle vegetation, but finding water was our reward. When I first saw the flooded parcel of land, all I could think of was cooling down and rinsing off the dirt. My fatigues were soaked from the sweat and humidity, and so were everyone else's.

Schmitt led the parade to take advantage of the water. His buzzed blond hair was covered in a layer of fine jungle dirt, making his head look like it had been peppered. When he pulled his helmet off and tried to shake it free, the dampness made it stick and the only thing that flew was sweat droplets. Brushing dirt from his fatigues with his grime-coated hands only served to add to the mess. This was a guy who aced every inspection, so we all kind of chuckled watching him attempt to look decent. Even covered in dust, though, he was the cleanest-looking guy in the unit.

I liked Schmitt, who had grown up on the south side of Chicago near where I was born, but I liked teasing him more. Besides Waite, I wasn't the scrawniest guy in the group next to Schmitt. Having someone smaller I could pick on, I never missed the opportunity. I made up nicknames with his last name—schmutt, schmuck, you get the idea. One day he was standing shirtless in the barracks, and I noticed he had a Marine Corps tattoo. I addressed him as Marine Schmutt, but before I could continue teasing him, he politely asked me to stop with the names. He said he'd had enough of it.

I was stunned at the request but decided to respect it; had he been an ass, I would have kept going. But his respectfulness took the energy from my jokes. So, I asked him about the tat instead. He told me he had been in the USMC before, that he got a hardship discharge when his dad passed away and he needed to take care of his mom. The military was in his blood, so when he got his mom back on her feet, he returned to the USMC and applied for jump school. The Marines said no, but the Army said yes. So here he was with the Army Airborne.

I trudged through the rice paddy behind him as my nose hairs curled at the smell of fish, mud, and dead flesh, possibly human. I gagged as I realized I was also smelling shit. I was opening my mouth to razz Schmitt when water splashed into it. It tasted as bad as it smelled.

Holding my M79 over my head to keep it dry, my arms trembled as I continued to wade through, going as fast as the mud would allow me. It wasn't long before I was ready for dry land to rest my arms and legs.

Glancing up at my M79, I saw a chopper coming in for a landing. It amazed me how sometimes you wouldn't hear them until they were right on top of you. They would fly close to the treetops, giving them the advantage of being quiet until they were ready to be seen.

The chopper took seven soldiers who were too exhausted to continue back to Củ Chi. These guys had overheated in the desert-like temperature, and the paddy water did nothing to help them. Left behind, I enjoyed the breeze—even if it was short lived—that the Huey blades whipped up as the chopper took off.

A little past the rice paddy, we found a spot where we would dig in for the night. I was more than ready to drop gear and dry my feet and boots. Little did I know that my feet wouldn't be dry for months.

In the distance, we could hear Sergeant Coy pushing the other guys to go on, especially his squad, but he acted like a sergeant with everyone. Like Ruper, this wasn't Coy's first time in Vietnam. His story—and the dramatic way he related it—had circulated throughout the whole platoon. I wondered if the entire battalion knew it too.

Coy grew up in West Virginia, and he had forged his papers to get into the Army. His older brother was going in and Coy wanted to be with him. The Army had a buddy system that worked well for brothers; they were able to train together and deploy to Vietnam together. Coy said he thought they would live for decades and die as old men. But Coy's brother got shot in-country and killed, and Coy had a front-row seat to his death.

He told the story with vivid details. Not only did his eyes get wide and glazed as he zoned out, falling back in time, but his pupils expanded, making his blue eyes even darker. Because he was so pale, he looked almost ghost-like, except for his eyes.

Coy got shot during the same battle, in his stomach. He lifted his shirt to show the scars for emphasis. The wound appeared horrific, and according to Coy, it was life threatening.

"I lost eighteen feet of my intestine," he said, almost bragging.

Assuming he was dead, the Viet Cong had left him alone. Coy cackled as he told it, saying he couldn't believe his fucking luck that those sons of bitches walked right over him. He said he didn't move a muscle as they kicked him and trampled on him like roadkill.

"I deserved an award for that performance," he smirked. "It was my best yet."

When the jungle went quiet, and he knew the "fish heads" were gone because he didn't hear their "Ching-Ching talk," he sat up.

Here he reenacted how he looked down and saw his guts hanging from his body.

"I shoved what I could back inside and grabbed a helmet to hold them in. Then I crawled over to my brother."

He said that everyone was dead, and that the hope that his brother was faking quickly faded as he moved the debris and saw that his brother's face was half gone, along with his left hip and leg. He first lay next to him, planning to die.

"Then a fireball shot through me and I sat up. I promised my hero that gooks would pay for what they'd done. Then I crawled until I found help."

Coy told that story over and over, and he always ended it the same way: telling us that we'd better never complain that something was too hard.

The first time I heard him tell it, intense fear overtook me. I'm not sure if it was because of the story or the way he told it; all I knew was, I didn't think it was bullshit. Coy was my age but he looked much older, partly because his thin hair made him look bald, and perhaps partly because of what he had already seen.

Before we left Fort Campbell, he got lectured by Captain Pritchard. The captain always told us that if we got into trouble, he'd better hear it from us before he heard it from anyone else. Captain Pritchard had two men, at two different times, call him about their pregnant daughters, seeking to make the father—presumably Coy—responsible. When confronted, Coy, with a smirk on his face, stated he didn't see any problem at all, that he'd marry them both. Snickers floated across the platoons, but Captain Pritchard was not amused. Coy became known for lacking respect or concern. Maybe almost dying does that to a man.

CHAPTER THREE

JUMP TO IT

MY FATHER AND BOTH grandfathers were all military men, so I felt like joining the Army was in my blood..

Just out of high school, I was hired on with the Frisco railroad. I worked alongside a man named Jim McMillan, who people referred to as a hero. He told story after story about his time during WWII with the 101st Airborne, and I hung on every word. I'd daydream about being called a war hero, especially around my friends. The very idea of it made me feel proud.

When I decided that I didn't want to wait for the draft, I encouraged my friends to join me in signing up voluntarily, but none of them would go. I couldn't understand why someone would want to avoid the military. Some guys were going to get married, and one guy said his dad would take care of his draft card for him. I just shook my head in response.

When I walked into the draft-board office to inquire about when I would be called up, the girl seemed surprised. Staring at me with false eyelashes so heavy that she looked sleepy, she told me the date was soon. Her shirt with a dizzy psychedelic print, and her mini-skirt miles away from her knee-high boots, distracted me momentarily.

"I like having things planned," I told her, regaining my focus. "Can I pick my date?"

Her eyes grew wide again. "Sure," she said, sizing me up as if I were crazy. "As long as it's within the next six months."

Weeks later, on February 17, 1967, Dad gave me a ride to my physical on his way to work.

"Don't get scammed by the card games they'll be playing in the barracks," he said. "Just hang back and don't get involved."

I nodded but was too nervous to pay much attention as he warned me about other things I was in for. When he dropped me off, it was so early that the doors weren't even open yet, so I sat and waited in excitement of what I was about to become.

I quickly found out that my dad knew what he was talking about. I hadn't been at Fort Leonard Wood an hour that night when the card games started. Not playing allowed me to watch how the guys were cheating and hustling the non-suspecting new soldiers out of their money.

The first night at Fort Leonard Wood, we stayed in barracks built in December 1940. I liked the feel of them, knowing they were like what Mr. McMillan had stayed in too. Unfortunately, they moved us to newer barracks the next night, which felt more like a college dorm than the Army. This was where I had my first shaving experience—not my head, but my face.

I had never shaved before, and standing in formation early that next morning, the drill sergeant saw the peach fuzz glistening. He yelled so close to my face that his spit stuck to my fuzz, and I couldn't help inhaling it as I breathed.

"You'll dry shave as punishment later today!" he announced.

I wanted to respectfully tell him that I had never shaved before, but I knew enough to stand tall, shoulders back. "Thank you, sir!" I said.

As soon as the word "sir" left my lips, his hot breath blew against my face and his screaming burned my ears.

"Are you a fucking moron? You don't address me as sir! I'm a First Sergeant and you will address me as such. I'm not your friend and 'Sarge' is not my nickname. You got that, asshole?"

I never made that mistake again, nor did I ever skip shaving.

After the First Sergeant's tirade, Allan Kuhlman snickered beside me. At that moment, he became my first Army friend. About the same size as me, with sandy brown hair and a wide contagious smile, Allan was quick-witted like a stand-up comedian. People tended to gather around him because he was always telling jokes. Lucky for me, we trained together all the way up until we left for Vietnam. When we weren't training together, we found ways to have all kinds of fun.

At Fort Leonard Wood my ASVAB (Armed Services Vocational Aptitude Battery) results implied that being a light-vehicle mechanic would suit me. As the Sergeant was conveying this to me, I could hear my dad's voice: *John, being a mechanic is a wet, dirty job.*

"Could I go to jump school instead?" I interrupted.

The Sergeant's bushy eyebrows moved like caterpillars. "Can you go to jump school instead?" he repeated. With a huff, he swiped the paperwork from the center of his desk to the edge, then he wadded it into a ball and chucked it into the trash can. He slapped a new blank form onto his desk and feverishly started filling it out, presumably so that I wouldn't have a chance to change my mind.

Unbeknownst to either of us, after the Sergeant honored my request for infantry, Kuhlman signed up for jump school too.

"If I don't go to jump school," he told me, "I'll probably end up with misfits who'll get me killed."

That echoed my thoughts that the Airborne crew were heroes.

With basic training wrapped up in May 1967, Fort Gordon was next. Between graduation and reporting, I was able to make a quick trip home to St. Louis. I had missed my family and my girlfriend, Rita—and I liked Kuhlman so much that I brought him with me. I thought having him as my brother-in-law was a swell idea, so I introduced him to my little sister, Janet. On our double date at the drive-in theater, Rita whispered in my ear that the new couple was kissing in the back seat. I gave a thumb up, thinking my plan had worked.

While my matchmaking skills seemed spot-on, all my soldier training went in one ear and out the other when we showed up at Fort Gordon. Dressed in civilian clothes, I drove my car onto the fort and pulled up right in front of the company commander's door. I prided myself on being punctual, and we were right on time.

I pulled open the screen door and sauntered into his office while Kuhlman waited his turn outside. I felt like I was oozing coolness as I told him I was Private Stillman reporting for duty.

Calmly, without even looking up, he said to me, "Do you remember how you are to address an officer?"

I felt fear rush through me and muttered a meek "yes."

"Oh," he continued, "so you remember that you're supposed

to salute? Walk back out that door and let's do this right." I was frozen. "Now," he said a little more loudly.

Hustling out, I found Kuhlman leaning against my car and chuckling. I punched his arm, turned on my heels, and went back in, doing exactly as I had been told.

I thought the worst was behind me, but then he asked, "Whose flashy car is out there with the chrome reflecting the sun into my eyes?"

My shoulders relaxed and a huge grin spread across my face. "It's my 1960 Chevy Impala," I said, puffing out my chest. "I picked red because it's my favorite color, and you should get a load of the horsepow—"

"I'm not talking about how I like the car," he interrupted. "I'm telling you that it isn't allowed on the fort. At all."

I could hear the agitation in his voice as he continued.

"You need to remove it . . . if it was gone yesterday, it would've been too late. Are you tracking me, private? Don't ever bring it back on the fort. Call someone and have it picked up."

I walked out feeling like the biggest fuck-up. Some soldier I was becoming, screwing up the most basic shit. I drove out the main gate and found a civilian lot right outside the fort. I could keep my car parked there for a dollar a week, so I eased it into an empty spot and lied to the commander, telling him I called my father to come get it and that he was on his way as we spoke. I might not have earned any bonus points that day, but I also wasn't about to part with my new showboat.

Having a car ended up making me quite a bit of cash by hauling guys around. In fact, my makeshift taxi service enabled me to never have to touch any of my paycheck. What's more, I sometimes got a mini vacation out of it. One time, Kuhlman asked if I and another guy would take a group of seven to Myrtle Beach, South Carolina, promising me a big payout. I had no idea how long the trip would be, and it turned out that all our money got spent on gas and beer. So after making the seven-hour trip, we had no cash for a hotel. Laughing off our plight, we played all day on the beach, then spent the night on the sand. We were underage, drinking too far from the fort, and we didn't give a damn—until my party in the sun left me with a blistered back and shoulders. That Monday, we had to head out for bivouac where we would spend a week simulating the conditions of Southeast Asia, which included no showers.

I knew to keep my mouth shut; the sunburn was considered destruction of government property, and the penalty was an Article 15. They would either take twenty-five dollars of the seventy-five I was making each month, or they'd take rank—and I didn't have any rank to take away, so I sucked it up.

All wasn't lost, though. All my life, we couldn't afford what my parents deemed luxuries, and one of them was deodorant. I was always a stickler about being clean, and I hated that the kids in school nicknamed me "Stinky Stillman." So when another soldier named Alfred pulled out his can of Right Guard, I asked if I could use some. He gladly obliged, then told me the PX—the military department store—had it. I loved the manly scent, and it quickly became my favorite. I couldn't wait for Rita to smell me wearing it.

Fort Gordon was overcrowded, but the Army used that to their advantage. The mess hall couldn't even begin to hold everyone, so we lined up, arm's length, at parade rest. Our feet had to be shoulder-width, hands clasped behind our backs, upper bodies at attention. The sergeant at the door would yell out "Give me!" as a warning to pay attention, then "Five!" which meant five men had to leave, and five would go in to eat.

To make it even more of a challenge, there were monkey bars at a certain point in the line. If you got stopped there, you hung on the bar above you, keeping the same arm's-length space. If you fell, you went to the end of the line—and not with the group of men you were training with, and who you were required to eat with. In other words, falling meant not eating, so you hung on.

When you got to the door, you had to know what letter you were, phonetically. If you didn't know you were Alpha, Bravo, Charlie, Delta, etc., you went to the back of the line, which again, meant not eating.

Once you made it into the mess hall, talking wasn't allowed. All you heard was the sound of silverware clicking against metal trays. And because we knew that someone was hanging on the monkey bars, we woofed our food as fast as possible.

Though it seemed harsh, I loved every minute of the structure. What I didn't love was being told that I was a fucking dud, that I would be the first one sent home in a body bag, that I wouldn't make it a week in the jungle. I could feel my blood boil every time they yelled that at me, so I pushed harder.

We left Fort Gordon by bus with orders for Fort Benning, Georgia. I thought I'd get a week's leave in between to go home, but no such luck. I mentally waved out the bus window at my car sitting in the parking lot, figuring it would be safe. I'd paid the lot fees for the month and expected I'd be back in three weeks.

At Fort Benning, we had no time for anything but training. In fact, we could never stand still or walk; we had to run everywhere or jog in place. Smoking was highly encouraged too. If you didn't have a cigarette, they told you to bum one. So much for logic when it came to physical fitness.

But I didn't care. I loved jumping from the towers, and even more from the planes. I felt like we were being made the best of the best, and nothing was going to stop me from achieving that status. When I was told at graduation from jump school that I had made the 101st Airborne, I knew I had made it.

The only thing that concerned me was my car. They had not only added a fourth week onto our training at Benning, but they promptly sent us to Fort Campbell after graduation, again with no leave. After a week at Campbell, knowing my lot fee was late, I got up the nerve to ask Sergeant Ruper for a ride back to Gordon. I didn't think he'd rat me out about my car, and I was right.

"How 'bout you pay for gas one way," he said, "and I'll make a trip of it with my wife."

I smiled. "Sounds great. But at least let me pay for gas for the round trip."

Ruper slapped my arm in fun and smiled back. "No need."

I just shook my head. That Ruper was one stand-up guy.

CHAPTER FOUR

RENDEZVOUS
WITH DESTINY

FORT CAMPBELL, located both in Kentucky and Tennessee, is home to the 101st Airborne Division. It opened November 15, 1941, the same day the Japanese Imperial Fleet was leaving the home waters of Japan for the attack on Pearl Harbor.

The 101st Airborne, known as the Screaming Eagles, has a shoulder patch of a black shield with a white American eagle, and a tab that says "Airborne" sits directly above the shield. When I was given mine, I realized it was the same patch that my coworker Jim would have worn, and it made me feel aggressive, defiant, physically fit, and eager to fight. The amount of pride I had for being part of America's greatest warriors was huge. In my mind, training was over. This was it.

I was wrong.

In our first formation at Fort Campbell, the southern August air swelled around us and we had to squint against the sun that shone brightly in our eyes as Captain Pritchard addressed us.

"You are now the 1st Battalion of the 502nd Infantry, Bravo Company. You are first strike." He strolled stiffly up and down the line as he bellowed, "You are America's finest. You are General Westmoreland's boys. None of you are going to Vietnam . . ."

Here he paused so long that I wondered what was up.

". . . as individuals," he continued. "The whole division is being called up. We are no longer sending guys as replacements . . . we'll hold you back and build up the division. Is that clear? You will train as an individual, a squad, a platoon, a company, a battalion, an entire division."

Of his entire speech, the word Vietnam was what stuck in my mind. Up until then, everyone else called it Southeast Asia. I remembered when I first learned about what was going on over there, back in 1963. An upperclassman had been killed, and the school had an assembly where they put a plaque in the sports case in honor of him.

When I told my mom, she pulled out the *World Book Encyclopedia* and together we learned about the small country on the map where so much unrest seemed to simmer. She said she hoped I never had to go; I remember thinking it was okay if I did.

It was after this first formation that I learned from Kuhlman that he was being taken out of infantry. He was still with the 101st, but now, after all our time together, his training would be different from mine. To say I was disappointed would be an understatement.

When I got my first free moment, I set out to find my old friend Bill DeArmond. Bill and I met in second grade, and he lived down the street from me. He joined the Army eight months before I did and sent me letters all through his training, so I knew his address at Fort Campbell.

When he opened the door, he was shocked to see me, standing there in my uniform. He invited me in and we immediately began catching up, which led straight to exchanging car stories.

I regaled him with tales about my Impala—about my run-in with the company commander at Fort Gordon, and how my first order of business at Campbell was to find out what was required to keep my car on the fort.

He laughed. "At least you've got your priorities straight."

"That's right," I said, laughing with him.

"So what'd you have to do so they'd let you keep it?"

I chuckled. "Here's the good part. It failed the safety inspection because it didn't have seat belts. So I went and bought some, then fastened them in using wire hangers. They never would've saved a life, but they got me through that inspection."

Bill threw his head back in another hearty laugh. "That's a good one." Then he tossed his head toward the door. "You gotta see my beauty."

We walked a short distance. "There she is," he said, extending his hand toward his '67 Chevy Camaro. It was a deep maroon, reflecting the setting sun.

"Nice," I said. "You get to drive it much?"

"All the time. The trip home's a breeze. I'm going this coming weekend if you want to join me."

I was more than ready to see my parents and my girl, so I eagerly said yes.

Bill and I started making weekend trips, trading off who drove each time. Obtaining a pass off base meant standing in line for two hours or more, and it was only good for forty miles anyway, so Bill and I ditched the formalities and took our chances. We relished those short weekend getaways, but we were only able to make a few before Bill got his orders to go to Vietnam. I was confused at first because I thought we were going as a division. But together we made the assumption that his MOS—military occupational specialty—had a slot that needed to be filled. Later, I found out in a letter that once he arrived in-country, he was put with the 173rd Airborne.

Without Kuhlman to train with, or DeArmond to share the ride home each weekend, it felt a bit lonely. With guys being regularly shipped off without much warning, I hoped the pattern of losing friends didn't continue.

Despite the absence of two of my best friends, Fort Campbell did have its perks. The biggest was that I could drive home in five hours, and alone to boot. Even though I was technically A.W.O.L. with or without a pass, I continued to take my chances the way Bill and I had.

On my first few trips, I was practical: I left St. Louis to get back to Campbell at a decent hour. With each trip home, however, my return trip stretched later and later. It got to the point where I was walking into the barracks as the lights were turned on to wake everyone. I'd strip off my civilian clothes and replace them with fatigues. Training would be so intense on Monday that I'd skip supper, go straight to the barracks, and crash for the night.

The mood around Campbell from the very start was different from any other fort. The soldiers kept more to themselves; we had a bond in training, but we didn't get to know each other on a personal level. That was probably because I wasn't spending my free time with the guys—instead of offering taxi service like I had at Fort Gordon, I was training and sneaking home.

Even though I wasn't forging as many friendships, some guys stood out more than others. One was a guy named Oswald

Vile, who we called Big Old Vile. He looked like a lot of body compressed into a short, stocky square, and his balding head made him look older than everyone else. He chewed on a stubby cigar and was always getting into trouble. At first, I thought Sergeant Allen was constantly screaming, "Pyle! Pyle! Pyle!", as if he was making fun of him as a goof-up, like Gomer Pyle. Later, I found out he was actually saying "Vile! Vile! Vile!", which wasn't much better.

Breaking rules meant being put on detail duty in the barracks, where you buffed the floor in socks all day long, eight hours at a time. You had to ensure the twelve-foot aisle was polished to a high shine, using a wool Army blanket under the polisher to keep the buffer from leaving marks, so that the dark green marbled tile was mirror-like. It probably goes without saying that the buffer ran whether the floor needed it or not. Lucky for me, I never got in trouble. Vile was in trouble enough to keep that floor polished for everyone.

In the first platoon bay, we also had two twenty-gallon galvanized trash cans, and someone had had the job of polishing them with Brasso until they shined. They sat upside down at the end of that gleaming aisle, with the lid sitting on them, so there was no chance of anyone throwing trash in them. A large red heart was painted above the cans, which was the symbol for the 502nd. I chuckled thinking it was a reminder that if you loved your platoon, you didn't dare smudge those cans.

Each bunk had two lockers, one for military and one for civilian. The contents of the military lockers in that bay were identical; you could open each one and couldn't tell them apart. The civilian lockers held different items, but the order was neat, hangers spaced. We had foot lockers too—we were told what had to be in there and how it had to be placed, but the items never got used.

While we were required to keep everything in the barracks at its utmost tidiness, that center aisle was treated like a holy shrine. Only one person was allowed to walk down it: the company commander, Captain Pritchard. Everyone else avoided it. If you wanted to visit with the guy across the aisle from you, you walked all the way around. No cutting across, no stepping on it. When the captain would come in for inspections, however, he would scuff it all up. We all believed it was intentional.

One day, Vile was buffing the aisle and a private came running in, right down that freshly polished center. Vile cussed at him to get off it, but the guy said he was in a hurry. Vile charged him, grabbed his bicep, and in one swift move broke his arm.

"The next time it'll be your legs," he muttered, shoving him to the floor.

The tension around Campbell was high.

On November 5, 1967, one day before my twentieth birthday, I got orders that the division would leave for Vietnam on Monday, December 11—pushing things up a full six months ahead of schedule.

We weren't told why.

I was supposed to have thirty days of leave before that flight to Vietnam; my last had been right after I graduated basic at Fort Leonard Wood. That thirty days was out now, but I still took a trip home every weekend. As the departure date got closer, they quit issuing passes, not that I was getting them anyway.

On the last weekend before we left, my car broke down when I was taking Rita home—not a surprise as I hadn't done any service to the car in months. My dad came and picked us up, leaving the car in a parking lot. He later sent me a letter telling me he had the car towed to a mechanic, who said the spark plugs were all burnt up and the tires had had it. Dad paid to have it all fixed, and my sister Janet got to drive it the entire year I was gone.

My folks drove me to the Greyhound bus depot that Sunday. My two younger sisters, Janet and Linda, my little brother Gary, and Rita all came too. Easing silently out of the car, we stood quietly under the foreboding sky, crossing our arms against the damp cold. Depression carved lines in our faces as we looked at each other, then at the ground, then back at each other. Finally, Rita handed me a note.

"Don't read it now," she said, wiping a tear.

I stuck it in my pocket and hugged her. When I let go, she turned away, unable to look at me.

"Don't try to be a hero, son," my dad said, "but try to come home." He reminded me about the neighbor boy, Johnny Hofer, a Marine who went to Vietnam and came home with a medal for charging a bunker. There had been a big writeup in the local paper about it. "Don't think you need to be like him and do that," he said.

That thought had never crossed my mind. I figured I wouldn't have to worry about that kind of thing being Airborne. "Don't worry, Dad," I said.

He pulled something out of his coat and handed it to me. I took the army green book and saw that it had 1968 embossed on the front.

"You might need it to log and record things," he said.

I turned it over in my hand. I'd never had a pocket diary before, and I wondered if any of the other guys would have one. "Thanks, Dad," I said, tucking it into my bag.

My family all approached to give me one last hug. I swallowed hard then turned and walked up the steps to the bus.

Scanning for an open seat, I spotted Means sitting about halfway down. "What are you doing here?" I blurted out.

He told me he had been at his older brother and sister-in-law's house across the river.

"What are the chances?" I said, plopping down in the seat next to him.

After hours of chatting, Means drifted off and everyone on the bus grew quiet. I suddenly remembered the note from Rita. I pulled it out and squinted to read it in the dim light.

Johnny, remember darling, that I love you and I miss you so much. I will be here waiting for you. Hurry home.

I folded it back like it was, pressed it to my lips, and put it back in my pocket. It was going to Vietnam with me, and I planned on keeping it forever.

The last weeks at Fort Campbell were brutal. Not only was the training intense, but the guys started fighting each other. We had been living and training together for six months, and we had been geared to fight, to kill. We knew we had to do it, but we were stressed—about leaving loved ones, about going to Vietnam. As a result, we were turning on each other. To keep us under control, MPs guarded us 24/7, and they kept the two bay doors secured with a chain and padlock. They would unlock it to escort us to the mess hall to eat, then they would accompany us back to the barracks. The Army even took away all guns and ammo, bayonets, and anything that could be used as a weapon.

On Monday at midnight, white buses picked us up to take us to the airstrip at Campbell. We were dressed in full combat gear, minus the ammo. I figured they would pass out the ammo during the flight, since we'd have to go running out the back hatch and into the jungle, firing our weapons as soon as we landed. That shows you how little we were told.

Outside my window looked like a ghetto after riots. It hadn't just been our guys going stir crazy; it seemed everyone at the fort had lost their minds. Windows were broken, stuff was burnt, trash was everywhere. I wondered what the hell had happened. It looked like all the men had turned on each other and that was the aftermath, except for the bodies.

Around 1:00 a.m., we loaded onto a C141 plane—a tin can with jump seats. It was the same plane on which we had done all our training, and this felt like the night jumps we had executed. Everyone kept asking for the ammo, afraid we'd get to the jungle without any. I wondered if they would give me as much as I could carry, or if it would be rationed. With all the nerves buzzing about, the energy never calmed down on that flight.

As the plane touched down at Travis Air Force base in California, my heart skipped a beat. I had no idea what to expect, so when the tires skidded on the runway, it sounded like a crash. It was the first time I had ever landed in a cargo plane; on all the other flights I had jumped.

They herded us into the mess hall as the plane headed back to Fort Campbell for another load of soldiers. When I got to the front of the line, the cook asked me how I wanted my eggs. I laughed. Surely it was a joke; they never offered us a choice.

"I have no idea," I said.

"How about scrambled?" he asked.

"Sure," I shrugged.

At the Army mess hall, "scrambled" eggs were watery and splattered on a tray. But here at the Air Force mess hall, the cook gently spooned fluffy, buttery eggs on my plate. I couldn't help but wonder if I'd joined the wrong branch.

We waited at Travis for two hours, being told that the move was the largest and longest ever undertaken: more than 10,000 members of the 101st Airborne, 1,000 of whom had volunteered to return a second time to Vietnam, plus all our equipment. The Army called the move Operation Eagle Thrust.

Our next stop was Wake Island, located two-thirds of the way between Honolulu to the east and Guam to the west. The stop was to fuel up, but I was able to pick up some paper, pencils, and a postcard with a picture of Wake Island, which I sent to Rita.

From there, we flew through the night sky to the Philippines, where scores of Christmas lights reminded me of home. The sticky, hot air, however, told me I was a long way away.

I ate, shaved, and waited the three hours until we took off again.

Our next stop would be Biên Hòa, South Vietnam.

STIRRING UP
SHIT

ON DECEMBER 13, 1967, I stood in formation with the rest of the fresh soldiers at the Biên Hòa airbase. Clad in combat fatigues, we were told we were marking a new and potentially crucial phase in the war. General Westmoreland said the month-long secret airlift boosted the US strength to almost 500,000, and that with his boys over here, he knew he could wrap this thing up. I felt my chest swell as he talked about how we were the best. I looked at Cantu and saw his chest was puffed out too.

Cantu had been in the same barracks with me at Campbell. He was Latino, with coffee-colored skin, dark brown hair, and even darker eyes with bushy brows. The girls loved his exotic good looks, and his infectious personality and loud laugh drew people to him. For whatever reason, I hadn't spent much time with him until the day he walked into the barracks as I was tending to my new tattoo.

I had wanted an Airborne tattoo, and it killed me to wait until I was officially Airborne to get one. I had the artist ink a pair of jump boots with wings coming out the side and a parachute in the background, with "Johnny" arched over the top and the word "paratrooper" underneath. I chose red and turquoise to make it stand out.

When Cantu saw it, he gushed about how cool it was and asked if I would be offended if he got the same one.

"Not at all," I said. "I'd be honored if you had the name Johnny tattooed on your arm."

He let out a bold pelt of laughter.

Standing next to him now, with our matching tats under our fatigues, I thought of him as my tattoo brother.

After loading into Army trucks, we convoyed through Saigon. I was amazed at the old oriental buildings but disheartened by how dirty and primitive the city was. The sewage ran straight into the ditches, filling my nose with a mixture of truck fumes, shit, spices, fish, smoke from the cooking fires, and marijuana. I also noticed how the cars were just like those at home: a French Renault like my dad owned, several Chevys, a VW Bug.

A dirt road took us away from the city to Củ Chi, a suburban district of Saigon City, Vietnam. Củ Chi was a major US base camp, home of the 25th Infantry. Later it would be discovered that under Củ Chi was a complete city used by the enemy.

Sergeant Ruper told us it was known as the only place on earth where you could stand up to your ass in mud and still get dust in your eyes. With all the wind, one would think the air would be fresh, but the scent at the camp was as strong as the stench in Saigon.

As we unloaded the truck, it was easy to tell the new guys from the seasoned ones. Our faces were baby fresh, wrinkle-free, and wide-eyed, while the ones who had been there longer had a look of disgust on their faces, with a hint of sadness. Our fatigues were green and clean; theirs had a tint of red to them from the dust. We newbies smiled, laughed, and joked. The "veterans" growled, cussed, and frowned. I never thought I'd be like those guys. It never dawned on me that they had probably felt the same way when they got here.

My first week was spent working around camp, becoming familiar with and acclimated to the country. Every morning, in the dark, we would run the inside of the perimeter, up and down the roads like we did at Campbell, singing cadence as loud as we could about wanting to be an Airborne Ranger. The huts, with only screens for windows, hugged the roads we were running on, and the guys inside them would yell things like, "You idiots!" and "You're in Vietnam now. You'll see what you're in for!"

The Army had other ways of getting us adjusted too.

I had heard others talk about shit detail, but I didn't know they literally meant it.

The shitters at Củ Chi were outside—outhouses made from wood, with twenty to thirty toilet seats on a bench, so close together that you rubbed elbows with the person sitting next to you. A mama-san worked in each one, keeping the floors swept and the toilet paper stocked. She would walk the fifteen- to twenty-foot length, back and forth, asking if everything was okay. On the back side were trap doors for each toilet seat. When a door was opened, it revealed a fifty-five-gallon drum cut in half. When you had shit detail, this was your office.

Using a piece of rebar with a hook on the end, you'd reach in and drag that half-drum out, then quickly put a fresh, empty one in its place. It worked best to have someone upstairs guarding that particular seat so that no one used it while you were making the exchange. If someone went while you had the drum pulled out, you got to clean that up too.

If you timed it right, the drum would have twelve to eighteen inches of waste in it. We'd pull it away from the shit house, pour five gallons of diesel fuel in it, light it on fire, and then stir it continuously. It was like cooking, except it was horrible. They say smoke follows beauty, and I'll tell you, this was the time you wished you were ugly. The smoke would waft constantly into your face, and there would be four pots going all the time, day and night. Even with all the pot stirring, the latrine was almost always in a state of overflow.

We also had piss tubes all over the camp, each of which consisted of an aluminum canister that originally held a howitzer round. A bug screen sat at one end, and the other end was placed in the ground at a slight angle. For these, there was never a line, except on movie night. We all looked forward to when the supply sergeant would rev up the projector, throw up a sheet, and play a flick while serving ten-cent beers. We all made frequent trips to the piss tubes on those nights.

No matter how distracted we attempted to be with the films and singing and constant duties, however, we could hear the sound of battle all around us. The camp was getting mortared often, so there was never a time when we weren't in danger. What made it more poignant was that when we had to fill sandbags, we would be surrounded by children. It took our focus from the war sounds to hear their giggles, and we would always stop to play with them. Being in the presence of those innocent souls, I understood why we were there: they needed a better country, and my job was to give that to them.

CHAPTER SIX

A RAT'S LIFE

THE BATTALION DUG IN AS darkness fell on the jungle; the constant gunfire stopped when complete blackness took over. It should have been reassuring, but instead it made me nervous.

We were told not to sleep, to stay on guard.

I sat next to Jerry Boyer, another Missouri boy, who I met at Fort Campbell. He had the kind of baby face that made the other guys ask if he belonged in the Army. He'd just smile. He was career military, so he got a kick out of the ribbing.

Since we were both from the same state, we told people we were cousins. Why we did that I don't know, but I do know we had fun with it. Boyer was a few years older than me—he was twenty-three and I was twenty—and this was his re-up. He was also in B Company like I was.

On that night, he sat quietly next to me, focused on a picture of his wife and baby girl back at home, rubbing his finger over the picture as if they could feel his touch on their faces.

"I'm bummed we won't see Bob Hope," I said, trying to make conversation.

"Yeah," he agreed in a maudlin tone. "He's here for the other soldiers, not us fucking new guys."

Boyer was about five feet four, making him the perfect candidate to be a tunnel rat. The tunnels were left over after the Viet Minh fought the French. Ho Chi Minh, the leader of North Vietnam, ordered that the tunnels be maintained. Despite being cramped, narrow, and dark with poor air quality, they held a complete world: living quarters, hospitals, training areas, storage for ammunition. They were also home to snakes and rats—and the VC, or Viet Cong.

We would later simply call the VC "charlie." The shortening came because when radioed in, VC would be called out phonetically, which is Victor Charlie. To keep things easy and quick, GIs shortened it to charlie.

In the early-morning hours before the sun came up, C Company stumbled on a tunnel, and B Company was called to help them. Sergeant Coy was quick to volunteer Boyer.

I hated watching Boyer crawl down into the tunnels, but not as much as Boyer hated being a tunnel rat. He was only allowed to take a forty-five-caliber pistol, a flashlight, and a knife. When I'd hear him hit the bottom of the tunnel with a thud, I didn't know if I'd see him again. All we could do was wait.

On one of his first missions, he uncovered weapons and ammunition, which we confiscated. He had come up out of the tunnel temporarily deaf from firing his weapon in a small place, carping about how frightening it was in there, how dark and damp it was. The tunnels were so narrow that his shoulders touched the sides; some spots he would have to push himself through, causing the dirt to crumble. He told us how he stabbed at shadows that he thought were charlies, saw insects with pinchers big enough to carry him away, and dodged hanging snakes that the Viet Cong had tied to tree roots. Some tunnels were even flooded, so getting lost was a real possibility too.

Boyer told me that he dreaded being in those tunnels. Before long, we could hear him quietly crying at night, saying he didn't want to do any more of them.

We planned our R&R together to keep Boyer's mind off the missions. Married guys usually went to Hawaii, because it was easy for their wives to travel and see them, but Boyer's wife couldn't travel with an infant so he was going to Sydney, Australia, and I was going with him. Australia was the top pick, but unmarried, high-ranking guys were typically the only ones who went there. We heard stories about how Australian women loved American soldiers, that they would be waiting at the airport with signs, ready to wine and dine the GIs.

So even though Boyer was married, they were letting us both go to Australia—because we were cousins, or so they told us. Though R&R wasn't until April, talking about it kept us from worrying about what was going on around us.

We had been out in the field for days. The choppers were unable to get supplies to us, so we decided to pool our resources. One guy had sugar, another had instant-coffee packs, one had a package of hot chocolate, and another had a packet of cream. Between us, we had about a cup of water, so we decided to dump the coffee and hot chocolate into one cup and heat it all up together. It seemed like an odd combination at the time— this was way before it was a staple of every coffee house menu —and each of the four of us would only get a small swig, but that didn't matter. I salivated as I waited, thinking of how the sweetened-up coffee was going to taste.

When the brew was almost ready, Sergeant Coy sauntered over to see what was going on.

"What's this?" he asked slyly. He picked up the concoction and without hesitating, spit a loogie into it. His laugh was hearty as he walked away with our canteen cup, leaving our circle stunned.

We should have hated Coy. But besides ruining our cup of coffee, we liked him okay. Mostly, we were relieved that he wasn't our squad leader. He led his men with unbridled energy, always volunteering them for missions, leaving the other squads to rest, even if only for a short time. Because of this, Coy's men were always exhausted, while we often caught a break.

It was clear that Coy knew war and was after revenge. He always wanted to be first in—with his aggressive, almost enti-tled attitude, his squad would follow behind with tears in their eyes, tired of being first. Stories started traveling around the platoons about Coy's actions—how he was kicking the gold teeth out of the gooks he killed and keeping them in a little velvet bag. Word had it that he would spot someone with gold teeth, then kill him so he could have the gold. He had a small drawstring bag, made to hold loose tobacco, that he'd drop the teeth into, then discreetly send it home when the bag got too full. One of the guys said that Coy told his mom not to open the packages, to just place them under his bed.

If that wasn't enough, we got out of the village once and were waiting for the chopper in the open rice paddy when the last to walk out was Coy. I thought, *How'd he get to the rear?* He had been first, and now he was the last. Strutting toward us, he held that bag with the teeth and had blood on his face. When I asked him about the blood, he told me that he was cutting charlies' throats and drinking their blood. I just stood there stunned. I wouldn't have been surprised if it was true. Everyone called him Crazy Coy.

Soon after, we were humping through the jungle when we came upon an opening. It looked like a plantation out of *Gone with the Wind*. I blinked a few times, thinking I was seeing a mirage. These plantations were scattered across South Vietnam from when France was in power and produced the world's share of rubber. The old French colonial–style houses looked out of place among the otherwise primitive-looking homes scattered about the Vietnamese countryside.

The war had ravaged a large swath of this particular rubber plantation, and some of the acreage had not been reclaimed. A small group of Army Special Forces surrounded the perimeter of the house, and I could hear water splashing and the hollering of guys who were horsing around. The closer we got, the more I could see, and a swimming pool came into view with guys on a diving board. I couldn't wait to join them, and I didn't even like to swim.

But the excitement didn't last long.

"You're on patrol here, men," Sergeant Ruper barked. "No one's going into that house."

We exchanged looks of disappointment and a few audible groans filled the stifling air.

Vietnam had two climates, cold and wet or hot and dry. My body ached for the freshness of that swimming pool and the chance to take off my boots and dry my wet feet after a clean swim. But instead, we humped on, looking over our shoulders a couple times at what we didn't get to experience.

The rubber trees were planted with precision, leaving no cover at all. I would be protected from one angle, only for the rest of me to be completely exposed. The perfectly spaced trees reminded me of those carnival games where you aim a rifle at a row of ducks that pass by.

I was thrilled when we got away from that rubber tree farm. We had spent the whole day moving through a mushy, overgrown trail, with wind that constantly kicked up dirt, and my body was numb. When we got the order to rest, the hard ground was actually welcome.

Unable to completely relax, I leaned back on my hands and rubbed the heel of my boot back and forth in the dirt. As I pushed it deeper, I noticed the ground was hard and I wasn't gaining any depth. So I reached down and moved the dirt with my hands. At first, I thought the mud was as hard as concrete, but then I realized it *was* concrete. Shocked, I marveled that I had unearthed a dirt-covered road in the middle of the jungle.

"No wonder this hump is harder than some of the other ones," I announced. "There's a road under here! The concrete makes it less forgiving."

"Whoa," someone said. "The jungle's taking over!"

As the guys began murmuring around me, I tried to picture what the road was like when it was new, long before the Vietnamese had to fight for what belonged to them. But before I could think about it too hard, Sergeant Ruper gave the command to take off again.

Not long after, we came upon a bombed-out bridge—

there was no water, but a steep ravine. As we trudged down through it past the bridge, I felt like we had been walking forever without seeing anything significant. I wasn't the only one.

I heard someone ask for a pace count. A platoon's lives depended on knowing where they were if they needed to call in for air support (a strike, a medic, ammo, etc), giving coordinates at any given moment of the platoon on the map. One guy had the tedious and critical job of counting steps. Using a map and making notes along the way through the zigzagging jungle terrain, this person was essentially the troop's GPS.

After receiving the coordinates from the pace counter, Lt. Hale took the radio from Means, our radiotelephone operator (RTO). "I need spotter rounds at our location!" The radio crackled as he read the coordinates.

We heard the usual "Roger that" but saw nothing.

"Request it again," someone said.

Still nothing.

Sergeant Ruper and Lt. Hale studied the map in earnest. In their defense, it was highly challenging to keep track of where we were in the thick jungle, despite everyone's best efforts. Sergeant Ruper's frown lines grew deeper between his eyes, then he looked up at us.

"Well shit, we're in goddamn Cambodia. How the fuck did that happen?" He wiped his head and shook it as he clenched his mouth. "Turn around!" he said, waving his arm. "Go back."

Means and I grimaced at each other as we about-faced.

THE DAWN OF
1968

THE NEW YEAR RANG IN with a day off and a cookout. Being in Vietnam wasn't the best start to the year, but the end would be a lot better when I went home the following December.

I liked being back at Củ Chi; it gave me a sense of security. The base had a concentration camp–style fence, with barbed wire at the top, and the whole perimeter was a mine field. Armored personnel and tanks guarded it twenty-four hours a day, and the inside contained plenty of bunkers to provide shelter from the mortar attacks.

I also liked payday. I wanted the Army to put all my pay into savings, but they said I had to take some, so I took the smallest amount. I had thought about buying an expensive camera from the PX, but after setting money aside until I had enough for it—something that was instilled in me from my father—I passed on the camera and decided to buy Airborne pins for Rita, my two sisters, and my mom.

I still wanted the camera, but I also wanted to buy a new car. I was hoping to make a promotion to Spec 4, which would raise my pay to $300.00 a month. I decided I would treat my-self with the camera first, then make a decision about the car. Guys were receiving brochures in the mail, and some were even buying cars while in Vietnam. We were told we'd save a bundle by ordering the car ahead of time, and that when we got home, it would be at the PX waiting for us. It sounded like a sweet deal; I just couldn't decide between a GTO and a Chevelle, and I didn't want to buy a car without seeing it first.

But dreaming about my future car was quickly replaced by the realities of being in Vietnam. After a day of in-country training that turned out to be real combat, costing the battal-ion three men—two guys from A Company, and one from mine—we returned to the firebase to rest and process the losses. The chaplain addressed us solemnly, sharing that one of the guys died on his twenty-first birthday. I hoped that didn't happen to me on my twenty-first.

From then on, my mind was filled with images and sounds I couldn't shake: the blown-up helicopter, the dead bodies. My dreams were as vivid as the real thing, so it was rare that I wasn't haunted by it. During stand-downs, I had brief periods that were somewhat normal, where I had time to wash fa-tigues, write letters, and make entries in the pocket diary. The best, though, was when mail arrived. All of us were thrilled to get letters, and I always looked forward to hearing from Rita.

The next morning, I was on detail when they told us we were going out to kill Cong tomorrow. All through lunch, I sat with that thought, unsure how I felt about it. The mail arriving was a welcome distraction.

"Looks like two for you, Stillman," the delivery guy said.

I eagerly grabbed the letters, happy to hear from my parents, but deflated that the other wasn't from Rita.

Mom said that Dad had gotten tile laid in the basement, making it the perfect place for my homecoming party. I was pretty sure that Means, Kuhlman, and Boyer would come to it. I had wondered if I should invite Sergeant Ruper and Captain Pritchard too. Heck, if I had it my way, I'd have the whole company come to my party. I figured we would all go home together, so why not have everyone there?

Thinking about the party reminded me that I needed to ask Mom to send Kool-Aid packets. The water tasted like shit because we had to put purification tablets in it. One of the old guys told me the trick about sweetening the water with Kool-Aid, so I decided to ask Rita to send me some too.

As I was folding my letters to home, we were told to be ready to chopper out in case we were needed. I quickly addressed the envelopes and raced out to the pad, where we sat for over an hour, wondering if the Army forgot about us. Finally, they loaded us onto a truck and took us outside the base.

"We need you guys to dig a large hole for trash," one of the officers said. "You're going to fill sandbags too. Got it?"

As we agreed, I caught site of vendors lined up right outside the gate of Củ Chi. They were selling all kinds of items, and one in particular caught my eye: a satin coat with a map of Vietnam embroidered on the back in vibrant colors. I remembered being four and receiving a similar coat from my Uncle Bob, my mom's brother, when he was in Korea. It was black satin and had the Korean map embroidered on the back in those same bright threads. I wore that thing until nothing was left. I knew my little brother Gary would love the Vietnam one, and I was able to quickly sneak away and buy it. I carefully slid it into my rucksack as I thought how I couldn't wait to send it to him.

As we got farther away from the base, groups of kids about six or seven years old ran alongside and behind the trucks, screaming with excitement. They swarmed us as we jumped from the truck beds, shoving items into our hands: Cokes, watches, cigarettes, clothes, liquor. "Buy!" "Buy!" they chanted. Kids selling cigarettes was a sight to see, but I was shocked when I saw that they smoked them too.

The military police were positioned to keep the aggressive kids back. They would push them away from the soldiers, but as fast as they steered ten kids away, ten more would run up to us. The scene matched the way sand filled the holes we dug as quickly as we scooped it out.

But even with the chaos and cacophony that surrounded us, that day felt like an easy one. I enjoyed watching the kids and knowing that I was going to make Vietnam better for them. I think we played with the kids more than we filled sandbags.

As we loaded back into the trucks, Sergeant Ruper told us that we'd only stay at Củ Chi for thirty days. After that, we would move to a new area to establish our base camp. He also said that we would start a ninety-day mission to take out the Viet Cong before the monsoon season started. I was pretty sure I could handle ninety days.

"During the recent briefing," Ruper added, "I was informed that some of you would be transferred to the 173rd Airborne, known as the Herd. They have more experience than you do, and the Army wants to mix the inexperienced in with them."

Hearing that made my heart sink. I didn't want to leave the 101st, but if they chose to send me, I figured I'd at least see DeArmond.

The following day, we went to the Ho Bo woods to check out tunnels. We didn't see any VC, but about ten of our men from D Company were shot. We had to stay out that night on watch. We couldn't see them, but the VC shot at us, and we shot back. Upon inspection the next day, we didn't find any dead bodies, but the battalion conducted a combat assault. We choppered out further into the woods where both A and B Companies discovered numerous booby traps, with fresh signs of VC.

Ho Bo was thick with bloodthirsty mosquitos, and the repellant the Army issued us was stinky and oily. It clogged our pores and made us feel hotter, so I kept a bottle in the band on my helmet and used it only when I was desperate. During the day, we could roll up our sleeves, but at night we had to roll them down and button up our collars—despite the stifling heat—so the mosquitos could only sting our heads and hands. It made using the repellant more tolerable because you didn't have to use as much, but it was miserable either way. All through the night, in our poncho tents, we'd hear them buzzing around.

The morning of the 4th came quickly without any of us getting much rest. The radio reported that Alpha and Delta

Companies had taken rockets in their perimeter during the night, so Bravo was instructed to head back to the area where the VC were encountered the day before.

We walked the woods in a V formation, like geese fly, with one soldier walking point as the first man in the combat infantry patrol. That day might have been my first time walking point—though it was rare for the M79 to do it—but it wasn't my last.

No matter my position, I had to stay alert at all times, but when in point, I was responsible for every goose behind me, so I had to be ready to react to unexpected attacks. Thankfully, because it was such a dangerous position, the Army rotated it. Though medics and RTOs never walked point, the Army made sure the rest of us had an equal opportunity to die. I couldn't help envisioning the worst outcome whenever it was my turn.

On that particular day, my company had it easier than the others until C Company made heavy contact and we went to help them. They called in gunships and artillery for support, and Sergeant Coy yelled something about no rest for the wicked as he fired his gun. He seemed so elated about the contact, his adrenaline was contagious. But nearly as soon as we arrived, the firing stopped. It grew so quiet that I wiggled my fingers in both ears to make sure I hadn't gone deaf.

In what had seemed like only minutes, C Company was left with ten guys wounded, seven killed, and one missing. Gunpowder has a burnt smell to it and so does flesh. The scent made my eyes water as I trod through the jungle growth, some covered in blood, to help retrieve the bodies.

It would take at least six of us to move a body. The first

few I couldn't look at. It was too hard to see the mangled faces, or missing body parts. As I carried my comrades away from the massacre, I wondered how many dead gooks were on the other side of the combat zone. *Did we kill more than them? Would each battle do this to us?* I tried to do the math. At this pace, a company could be wiped out quickly. Body count was important in Vietnam, and we wanted to make sure our scorecard stayed loaded.

We cleared the area of all the wounded and killed, but we still couldn't find the missing guy. Before long, choppers came and airlifted us out of the woods. Afterward, the Army called the 11th Cavalry, the Blackhorse Regiment, to come in to level the area with tanks. Taking it to dirt, they stripped the jungle vegetation and removed refuge for the enemy.

I liked the 11th Cavalry. They rode in the APC—armored personnel carrier—and the back was packed full with ammo and C-rations. I thought it would be good to be one of those guys. Later, I would learn how their transport was nothing but a large, noisy target for the enemy.

On that chopper ride back to Củ Chi, I thought about how I was determined to go home alive, not to be returned to my family in a body bag. With what I had seen up to that point, I was beginning to think it might be harder than I could have imagined.

"It's better to get killed early," some of the old guys said. "Then you're done and out. It's worse to get six months in and get killed."

I still thought it might be best to not get killed at all.

JANUARY 5, 1968

WE STAYED IN BASE CAMP TODAY. I HAD KP AND WHEN I GOT OFF I WENT TO THE SHOW. IT WASN'T ANY GOOD SO I WENT BACK TO THE HUT. I WROTE RITA AND HOME AND THEN WENT TO BED.

JANUARY 6, 1968

WE STAYED IN CAMP TODAY AND GOT READY TO GO OUT TO THE WOODS. AFTER LUNCH I WENT TO THE PX TO PASS THE TIME. WE HAD CLASS TONIGHT THAT LASTED FOR AN HOUR. I WROTE HOME AND BILL. I GOT TWO LETTERS TODAY FROM HOME.

JANUARY 7, 1968

WE WENT BY CHOPPER TO BIEN HOA. FROM THERE WE WALKED AROUND THE WOODS. WE WERE TOLD THAT WE COULD NOT SHOOT ANYONE UNLESS HE SHOT AT US FIRST. WE DIDN'T SEE ANY VC TODAY.

The next morning, Ruper gathered us up for instructions: we were going for a daytime jump. I was thrilled to be able to put on a parachute and do a jump like we did in training.

The parachutes are heavy, so you can't just walk around with them on. So we geared up, then sat on the tarmac. After an hour or so of waiting, we were told we weren't going, with no explanation why.

"We're going to have you patrol the area instead," was all they said.

With disappointment rippling through the entire group,

we stripped off the chutes and left them lying in a deflated-looking heap.

As I was walking away from my chute, I was shocked to see a buddy of mine from jump school. It had only been six months since I'd seen him, but it already seemed like years.

"Hey! What are you doing here?" I asked him.

"I went through pathfinder's school," he said, shaking my hand.

No one had ever mentioned that option to me, so I asked him about what he did. It sounded like a gravy job, and I actually considered asking to change. But like other military jobs I had misconceptions about, I would later learn that the Pathfinders were in just as much danger as I was. It seems there was no escaping a station in Vietnam where your life wasn't in jeopardy.

JANUARY 8, 1968
TODAY WE SAT IN THE WOODS WAITING FOR IT TO GET
DARK. WE WALKED THROUGH A VILLAGE AFTER IT GOT
DARK, AND THEN WE WENT TO THE RIVER TO SET UP ALL
NIGHT AMBUSH. NO LUCK

JANUARY 9, 1968
WE WALKED BACK TO OUR FORWARD BASE CAMP
EARLY IN THE MORNING, ATE CHOW AND THEN GOT BACK
ON CHOPPERS AND CAME BACK TO Cu Chi. WE
CLEANED UP AND GOT SOME SLEEP.

JANUARY 10, 1968
TODAY WAS LIKE EVERY OTHER DAY IN BASE CAMP. AS ALWAYS, WE HAVE SANDBAGS TO FILL. DETAIL TO PULL. I WENT TO THE SHOW TONIGHT AND WROTE A COUPLE LETTERS.

JANUARY 11, 1968
I STAYED IN CAMP TODAY AGAIN. WE HAD DETAILS TODAY AS WE ALWAYS DO WHEN WE ARE IN BASE CAMP.

The detail work at Củ Chi made it look better and better, but they worked us to death at base camp. Though it sounds crazy to say, I actually wished we were out looking for VC.

FIRST STRIKE

FOR WEEKS WHILE AT Fort Campbell, I would salute and say, "First strike!" It wasn't until I was in Vietnam that I learned the reason behind those words.

During the first month in Vietnam, we would load up on choppers, fly out to a spot, and take the leap. The first few times, we waited until the chopper was less than a foot from the ground, then jumped. As we grew more comfortable—and more brave—we jumped from higher altitudes. Of course, the adrenaline rush was more intense the higher up we were, but I loved the chopper rides no matter what level we were at. That feeling of sitting at the door, having my feet on the runner or my legs dangling, my ass on the edge—there was nothing like it.

The captain and the RTO were always in the middle, which was considered a safer spot, so that meant Means sat there. After I saw that chopper shot down, however, I knew there wasn't a safe spot in the helicopter, or anywhere in the jungles of Vietnam for that matter.

We were often the first soldiers to an area, so we were the first strike. Depending on how many helicopters were flying, the first load would come in shooting. As standard practice, whether the door gunners could see the enemy or not, they would send a rain of bullets toward the right and left of that landing zone to secure the area, whipping up leaves and debris. The first few times, I assumed they were shooting at the enemy. I'd strain my eyes in the whirling dust to try to see what they saw. It was only later that I realized they didn't have to see a thing to shower ammunition over the area.

Once that first phase was carried out, the second and third loads would descend, which included me. Our guys would already be on the ground, having sprinted to the edge and created a perimeter around the landing zone. After we jumped from the Huey, we would run and spread out as fast as possible, sweeping an area to flush out any NVA—North Vietnamese Army—or Viet Cong. As twisted as it sounds, I always hoped someone would shoot at us. It made them easier to find.

More often than not we would encounter women in the villages, working like dogs with babies on their backs, or toddlers clinging to them. They were either toiling on farms—working the soil, planting, harvesting, and tending to the plants—or doing the washing, oftentimes in water that appeared muddy. Sweat dripped from their faces as they scrubbed the clothes, then twisted and hung them to dry.

Unless they were old, it was rare to see men. If they were of military age, they were off fighting; if they were VC, they were hiding in a spider hole or piles of hay, and we had to poke around trying to flush them out. When we encountered young men, we would insist on seeing their military card to prove they were only there on leave. If they couldn't show that, we knew they were charlie.

If there were too many gooks, we would call in artillery for support, and that sometimes included napalm—a mixture of plastics and gasoline that created a jelly-like substance that, when ignited, stuck to practically anything. It would burn for up to ten minutes, generating temperatures of 15 to 2,200 degrees. It was first used in flame throwers, then later as bombs that would destroy areas up to 2,500 square yards. I loved using napalm. It was the best way to quickly destroy anything around us that was a threat. I also enjoyed the smell. It almost gave me a high.

But I was amazed how much napalm could be used and we'd still have VC shooting at us. Our guys would drop a load of it, then wait. If we still had too many gooks attacking us, our backup would blast it again. This could go on for hours. My platoon and I would hang out in the rice paddies waiting for the word to go back in again.

Once cleared, our routine was to walk through a village, eliminate enemy fighters if we came across any, reboard the chopper, then fly to another spot to repeat the process. Operation Eagle Thrust brought thousands of eagles to defeat the charlies, but our goal was to appear so great in number that the villagers would tell others that they saw hundreds of thousands of men with white birds on their arms. Other villages would confirm seeing them too, sending a strong message that the charlies didn't stand a chance.

The Vietnamese had never seen an eagle, so they referred to us as the chicken soldiers, and they knew to avoid us at all costs. But the truth was that it was the luck of the draw during a sweep. One side of the company would hit land mines, while the other wouldn't see a thing. This ceaseless state of unknown was a constant reminder that I could never let my guard down.

JANUARY 14, 1968
I LEFT FOR THE HO BO WOODS TODAY BY CHOPPER.
WE AREN'T FAR FROM CU CHI. THEY SAID THEY HAVE
HEARD THAT THERE ARE BOO-COO VC IN THE AREA
THAT WE ARE IN. I DIDN'T SEE ANY VC TODAY.

The next day, I was given a flame thrower. I'd never used one, not even in training. They told me I was going to burn brush with it, and I immediately imagined myself in one of the WWII movies I'd seen, my excitement akin to receiving the greatest new toy as a kid. Only my excitement didn't last. My first time out, something ricocheted back into my eye, sending me to the hospital. Luckily, I only suffered dirt scratches; the doctor was able to fix me up with an eyewash and a pirate patch to wear for a few days. With the go-ahead for light duty, the Army had me guard the motor pool and supplies until I could return to my platoon. It felt just like being in the States on guard duty—I could hear bands playing, people talking loudly, and whooping and hollering. Being way inside the perimeter, I felt safe, so I wasn't worried or nervous. Plus, there were two of us, and no one came walking up until we were relieved of duty.

JANUARY 17, 1968
THE COMPANY IS OUT LOOKING FOR VC, BUT I AM AT
THE FORWARD BASE CAMP AND STILL GUARDING THE
SUPPLIES. THE GUYS CAME BACK TONIGHT, AND MY EYE IS
FINE NOW, SO I AM BACK ON THE LINE AGAIN.

The 501st, known as Geronimo, ran into some VC in the early morning on the 18th, but after walking about four thousand meters from our base camp, we didn't see any. I knew that if we did, they would be dead ducks.

JANUARY 19, 1968
THIS MORNING WE TORE UP OUR FORWARD BASE
CAMP TO GO BY TRUCK BACK TO Cu Chi. WHEN WE GOT
BACK I CLEANED UP AND WROTE A COUPLE OF LETTERS.
I WENT TO THE SHOW TONIGHT. WE LOST FOUR MEN
FROM A COMPANY AND ONE MAN LOST HIS FEET FROM
A MORTAR ATTACK

The following day, after another mortar attack that sent us scrambling to our bunkers, we were relieved to discover that no one was hurt. While I was on KP duty, though, a single gun shot rang out, and I ran from the mess tent to investigate. A guy lay writhing with a bullet hole in his leg. After they carried him off, the rumors started to fly.

"It was an accident. Happened while he was cleaning his weapon," some said.

"He shot himself intentionally so he could go home," others insisted.

I never did hear the true story.

Over the next couple days, we stayed fairly close to Củ Chi, spending some time at LZ X-Ray—the location of the first major air assault in Vietnam, and LZ Gold—which had been a hot spot for the 1st Cavalry in 1966. We knew that both were bad locations and were anticipating the worst, but while we did lose some men, it was not the kind of intense warfare we expected. The contact was light but frequent; D company lost one guy, and A company lost five more men in less than a month. It seemed our B company would be the lucky ones the whole time.

On January 21, we left Củ Chi and went up to the border of Cambodia, where we were told we would be gone up to ninety days—the ninety days Sergeant Ruper had talked about. Here is where we met up with the 11th Cavalry—the Blackhorse—who we would stay with until we returned to Củ Chi.

A few days later, after I'd barely escaped injury stumbling on a VC booby trap, we made a brief return to Củ Chi, where we were able to have a hot meal, a shower, and a shave—our first in five days. Cleaning up and eating a real meal would have been gift enough, but another was waiting for me: a box from my folks, with food and an Instamatic 100 camera. I wanted to mess around with the camera, but I only had time to wash clothes and pack my things because we were moving out the next day.

Our routine was to sit outside villages until dark then sweep through, with instructions to shoot anything that moved. Every time we liberated a village or hamlet that was previously under Viet Cong control, the Vietnamese returned to a normal life. A large part of that was being able to harvest rice from the paddies for their own villages and families, instead of for the enemy as they had been forced to do.

While we waited for the sun to fall under the horizon, we'd talk. Whenever you were crouched next to someone new, the first question was always, "How many days in?" We all knew the date we had arrived in-country, but I hadn't been counting the days. Once that became the answer everyone expected, though, I took a pen and marked the months on my helmet. When I reached the end of the month, I put an X through it. To be honest, each day felt like a blur, yet extremely long and individual too.

Mail took a while to catch up with us, and some guys had a hard time not getting any letters. I'll be honest, I did too. I worried about being forgotten over there. I begged Rita to send me a picture for good luck—I needed one to stare at when things got hard, and I wanted to get lost, however briefly, in what life at home was like.

On the 27th, we left Củ Chi by a C130 plane for the DMZ—demilitarized zone. We were joined with the 1st Cav, with not much else but a place to sleep—in a church of all places. That part of Vietnam was quite different from the South. There were a lot of hills, and the heat wasn't as intense, which was a relief we felt in every cell of our bodies.

That first week, we guarded the camp for the 1st Cav and set up bunkers. With the cooler weather and three hot meals a day, bunker guard felt like a cakewalk. When they choppered us out at the end of the week to take over for the 1st Cav, however, things changed.

Our first order was to check a village that had been bombed. Sweeping cautiously through, we found dead VC lying in twisted positions and guns scattered everywhere. Glancing around, we could read in each other's eyes that the

VC could be right behind us at any time. That week as bunker guard became a distant memory fast.

But then the mood shifted once again, in a direction we didn't expect.

They began sending us out by chopper to restore villages that had been destroyed by the gooks. As we entered a village, children would flock to us like flies to honey. We would smile and rub their heads playfully as they bounced around us, then they would watch with rapt attention as we spent the day digging holes and putting up cover. When we took a break, we would spend our time playing with the kids. Their mothers would watch from a distance, grateful but guarded. Looking at their children's faces, I could tell that they had only ever known war. *What a life*, I thought, *living and growing up in the midst of all that fear and violence.* I'd smile at them, hoping my gesture reassured them that we'd give them back a safe life, that we were showing them what freedom looked like.

That, I knew, made what I was doing worth it.

It didn't matter how many times I heard that I was a fucking dud, that I would be the first to be sent home in a body bag. Those words only served to fire me up. If someone told me I couldn't do something, no matter how impossible it seemed, I would do everything in my power to prove them wrong. And there in Vietnam, despite the danger and the heat and the fear, I felt like I was making a difference, that we were all making a difference, helping to take those people out from under the North's domination.

After we had restored a village, we would set up 200 meters away to observe if the VC returned and destroyed it. Sometimes they did. But when they didn't, I knew we were winning.

CHAPTER NINE

TET OFFENSIVE

ON JANUARY 30, 1968, both North and South Vietnam agreed upon a ceasefire in honor of Tet, the Vietnamese New Year. The holiday marked the beginning of spring for the natives; for us it meant downtime at Camp Evans.

From the evening of the 29th into the early-morning hours of the 30th, celebrations seemed to ring out from everywhere. Fireworks cracked open in the sky, and I imagined the Vietnamese happy that for at least a couple days, they didn't have to think of the war. Though my heart wanted to celebrate with them, I instead enjoyed the downtime.

Not wanting to miss out on the celebration, one of the guys went outside the gate and brought back bottles of whiskey.

"Don't open those!" someone said. "The enemy's putting glass slivers in the bottles."

"Oh, that's easy to detect," Coy said smugly. "You just pour some in your hand and rub it around. If there's any glass in it, your hand'll get bloody from the cuts."

Some of the guys tried that, but I didn't want to take any chances. I didn't like whiskey anyway, so it was easy to pass up. Quite a few guys got drunk on it, though.

The next morning, we headed out for patrol and stopped dead in our tracks. Highway One was littered with dead South Vietnamese civilians. We realized right away what it meant: the communist forces hadn't keep their word and had launched surprise attacks. The ceasefire that was to last for two days instead became a series of coordinated attacks on more than 100 cities and towns in South Vietnam. Thousands of unsuspecting citizens, who had reveled in the gift of celebrating their new year, had been blatantly slaughtered.

The following day, on February 4, we choppered out across the river to check out another one of the villages. We could see that the VC had been there, but not finding any right then, we made our nighttime position close to the village and settled in. Means and Legg were moved outside the perimeter to the listening post and were out there all night by themselves.

Around 3:30 a.m., we were startled by VC storming the area, attempting to get into our base camp. In the pitch blackness of the early-morning hours, the sound of gunfire became deafening from the other side of the perimeter. I couldn't get my bearings on how many were firing at us or from where, but I quickly pushed myself off the berm I was leaning against and prepared for the fight. Rubbing my eyes, I looked out into the rice paddy but couldn't see anything. It took a bit for word to make its way around the perimeter, but I had my M-79 poised and ready.

On the other side of the pagoda that stood in the middle of camp, the guys closest to the tree line of the village were taking the brunt of the attack. My mind raced, thinking we probably shouldn't have set up there but that now it was too late. The village had been empty when we passed through it the day before, but the fires from VC cooking rice still had embers glowing. I wondered as I heard guys scrambling awake to start shooting, *Did we unconsciously know we would draw them out to fire at us?*

"More ammo!" tore through the camp, not once but over and over.

Vile's voice was the loudest and I heard him most often. He carried the M60, an extremely heavy gun that was well suited to a guy his size. The front was equipped with a bipod that most men would have had to use as a stabilizer, but not Vile. His short, stocky body leaned so far forward that the force of the firepower kept him totally upright. When he reached my range of view, I could see him firing rapidly and chewing on his stubby cigar. He didn't stay long, though. It was only a few minutes before I couldn't see or hear him anymore.

Soon, choppers revved overhead and kicked out ammo. The boxes landed with a thud into the soft jungle soil, becoming enmeshed in the dirt and hard to pull out. In the pandemonium, word traveled that Means had been shot. I knew I had heard it incorrectly; as the RTO, they couldn't get to him. But what I didn't realize was that Means had been relieved of carrying the radio and was put on the M60 with Legg for an opportunity to move up rank to squad leader. Like a game of telephone, the story kept changing. First they said Means was okay, then thirty minutes later I was told he was dead. Then I heard Legg had taken shrapnel in the face and lost an eye, that a medic chopper had taken him away. That ended up being true, but I couldn't believe the last news that had circulated about my buddy, Means.

After the chaos of recovering all the ammo, Captain Pritchard gave the order to saddle up and move out. All I could think was that I wanted to get to Means. I didn't want to jinx him and tell him I heard he'd been killed. I just wanted to pat him on the back and see that he was okay.

I made my way through the vegetation, passing the battle-weary men with grime-encrusted faces, sweat streaking through the dirt on their cheeks like tears. When I got to the other side, I saw Means lying still on the ground. Not an ounce of blood was around him. I felt the breath escape that I had been holding; it was a relief to see him resting. I strained to see his chest move up and down, expecting him to sit up as I got closer.

But that didn't happen.

Shrapnel from an RPG had hit Means in the side of the neck. A hole that was barely the size of a pencil eraser marked perfectly where his life had ended. In this short time in-country, I had seen bodies blown apart, faces destroyed. In contrast, Means's face looked calm and peaceful. His wound seemed so minor, as if a Band-Aid would fix it.

I had broken the unspoken rule with Means, that we not get to know each other too well. I knew his first name, Ronnie. I knew about his family, his hopes, his dreams, his future plans. I knew how much he loved the Army, how proud he was of his accomplishments so far, how this would be his career.

With the demand for ammo gone, a chopper descended to take Means on the start of the trip home. He had lain there on the jungle floor for hours, devoid of life. Like me, he had wanted to be there, had felt there was a purpose in fighting. He had played with his green army men as a kid, but none of them had suffered the same outcome he did that day.

Still in shock, I helped to gently load him onto the chopper. It slowly lifted with a small wobble, then picked up speed as it began to thump through the fog. The blades seemed to slice the plans of a happy homecoming to shreds, telling me to bury the pain. I thought I'd cry, but I swallowed my pain like a good soldier.

From that point on, no one ever mentioned Means's name again, as if he had never existed.

Nothing had ever pierced my heart so severely.

There was no such thing as closure in war.

DOD Daily report.

5 Feb During the early morning hours the NDP [night defensive position] of Alpha was heavily engaged by a reinforced NVA company. Heavy contact from 03:26 hrs till 09:30 hrs, when enemy broke contact. Patrols were sent out to assess the situation. Contact made with estimated NVA platoon. 5 NVA KIA (BC). Company sized sweeps sent out resulting in heavy contact and 20 more NVA KIA (BC). Alpha and Bravo extracted. Delta made negative contact. Battalion set up NDPs around Quang Tri for the night.

Results:

Friendly: 33 WIA 1 KIA
Enemy: 0 WIA 25 KIA(BC) 100 KIA (estimated)
Captured: 2 MG's 2 AK-47 1 82mm and 1 60mm mortar

RONALD LEROY MEANS SP4 19 05-FEB-68 B CO

FEBRUARY 6, 1968
TODAY WE WENT BACK TO OUR MAIN BASE CAMP TO
SHAVE, CLEAN UP AND CHANGE CLOTHES. AFTER ABOUT
TWO HOURS WE WENT BACK OUT TO THE WOODS (FIELD).
WE CHECKED OUT A VILLAGE FOR VC BUT DIDN'T FIND
ANY.

FEBRUARY 7, 1968
TODAY WE GOT SHOT AT BY VC, BUT THEY DIDN'T HIT
ANY OF US. WE WENT INTO THE VILLAGE BUT DIDN'T FIND
ANY VC. WE WENT ON AN AMBUSH ON THE RIVER
TONIGHT AND GOT TWO VC BOATS.

We continued the search-and-destroy mission around Quang Tri, sweeping an area of the jungle that was so dense that at times I felt like I was tied up in vines—they would hold on so tight that I wondered if I'd know the difference if a gook grabbed me. Perhaps worse, even at the height of midday, the triple canopy above created a shroud of darkness.

The thickness kept the other soldiers from seeing me, but I couldn't see my fellow Army brothers either. Losing my sense of sight had me focusing on sound, relying on my ears to guide me from the spoken communication of the soldiers on each side of me. Like playing telephone once again, commands would be passed from one soldier to the next. We were separated by fifty feet and what seemed like over a thousand trees. When the hump first started, I wasn't sure who was on each side of me. It didn't take too many words, though, before I recognized Schmitt's voice.

"Stop!" he bellowed.

I was relieved and happy to hear his command and passed it to the soldier on my right, then sat down. The thick vegetation was so firm that it held me upright when I leaned against it. It was a perfect time for a smoke.

The noises of the jungle could be loud—birds, monkeys, and even insects all chattered to each other. Yet, with the abrupt absence of human conversation, I found it eerily quiet. I reveled in the short-lived moments before blowing out the last puff and "field-dressing" the butt, something that had been drilled into my head during training in the States. Nothing could be left behind for the enemy to find, so we had to tear the butt apart, remove the remaining tobacco, and make sure all the embers were out. This helped to keep the enemy from following us.

Stomping out the last ember, I was startled by gunfire. Hand grenades appeared to be coming from way out in front of us, but no commands had been given.

"What do we do?" I asked Schmitt frantically. I knew we were moving into a fight.

"No one's responding," he said.

In sheer panic, I turned to my right and yelled, not knowing if anyone was there or not, hoping for some guidance. When a voice spoke back, I recognized it: it was Waite.

"Is anyone next to you?" I asked. I knew that if there was, we'd be okay.

"No," he said. "It's silent." I felt my heart gallop faster.

I yelled for Schmitt and Waite to come toward me. I knew I didn't want to lose them. We were without a map or a radio, and we could walk right into the enemy. Standing still could get us killed too. We had no one guarding our rear. We needed a solution—and fast.

We had no idea if people approaching from behind would be American soldiers or the enemy, making any direction we went dangerous. As a threesome, we made the decision to go toward the gunfire. With slow, careful steps, we stuck close together and moved forward, knowing we could easily be mistaken for the enemy as we came up on our own men.

"I'm going to die," whined Waite.

My emotions were ready to explode, but I was trying desperately to hide my fear.

"Shut the fuck up," I yelled.

Of course he was going to die.

We all were.

I don't know if it was his insecurity that was pissing me off, or the fact that he was saying what everyone was thinking.

After a quarter mile of humping—fighting with the jungle as it tried to pull the weapons from our hands, stumbling over vines and roots, swatting bugs and dodging hanging snakes— we finally made it to the gunfire.

It was our company.

They didn't even know we had been missing.

FEBRUARY 8, 1968
IT IS STILL RAINING AND ALL WE DID TODAY WAS SIT
AROUND THE FIRE AND TRY TO KEEP WARM AND DRY.
WE MOVED OUR BASE CAMP ABOUT THREE HUNDRED
METERS AND SET UP FOR THE NIGHT.

During the night of February 8, the fog was so thick that you couldn't see your hand in front of your face. Suddenly, the NDP of A and B Companies were infiltrated by sappers—soldiers responsible for tasks such as building and repairing roads and bridges, laying and clearing mines, etc.—of the NVA. Explosions punctured the air as the soldiers on duty alerted the rest of us.

Sergeant Ruper was one of my partners in our four-man position.

No longer in the jungle, we quickly scooped out a hole in the sandy, dry soil, but we were unable to dig very deep because the soil kept washing back in. When the first explosion burst around us, I was on guard. I jumped into the hole, then two people jumped in on top of me and Ruper followed last. Finding it difficult to breathe, I was worried about being crushed to death. I was also worried about Ruper being on top. He was protecting me, but I knew it would be easy for him to be hit. We were essentially open targets, with nothing around to protect us. No canopy, very little vegetation, white sand like the desert.

When it was over, we discovered that A Company suffered six casualties from enemy contact. Waite was one of them. Because of the fog, we had no medevac or air support, so we sat with the bodies for several hours until the sun came up and the choppers once again had visibility.

Daily report.

Battalion continued search and destroy operations southeast of Quan Tri. Light contact was made during the day. Aerial

```
observation and other sources gave 1/502
credit for 250 NVA KIA (BC) for period 4 thru
the 8 Feb 1968

Results:

Friendly 82 WIA 12 KIA
Enemy 6 WIA/POW 305 KIA (BC) 100 KIA
(estimated)

During the night, Alfa and Bravo NDP were
infiltrated by sappers. Attacks very heavy.
Casualties 8 KIA 19 WIA 11 NVA KIA (BC)

Waite Donald Steven SP4 19  09-FEB-68 A-CO
```

In both companies combined, nineteen were wounded in action, one of whom was Sergeant Coy. With his zest for war, I imagined he was sent back home mad as a hornet that the enemy only suffered a loss of eleven.

Me? I was grateful to be alive, but I felt a wave of guilt wash over me for yelling at Waite when we were lost in the jungle. I also couldn't help but think about how he had prophesied his outcome so many months before it happened.

Once again, I didn't shed a tear.

OPERATION
SPREAD THE EAGLE

FEBRUARY 9, 1968
THIS MORNING AT 4:00 WE GOT MORTARED. THREE OF
OUR GUYS WERE HURT AND A CO HAD NINE KILLED. I WAS
REALLY AFRAID BECAUSE THEY WERE COMING IN CLOSE
TO ME. THE THREE GUYS IN THE NEXT HOLE WERE HIT.

FEBRUARY 10, 1968
THEY PUT US ON ROAD GUARD TODAY GUARDING
HIGHWAY ONE. IT IS A PRETTY GOOD JOB BUT I DON'T
KNOW HOW LONG WE WILL BE ON IT. IT IS STILL RAINING
AND I WOULD LIKE TO SEE THE SUN.

I KNEW THE 101ST WAS in Vietnam for the serious
business of helping a brave nation repel communist aggression.
I had wanted more than anything to be with the 101st, so I
naturally took great pride in the eagle patch I wore on my arm.
I was confused, though, when Sergeant Ruper handed each of

us a full sleeve of patches; none of us had that many fatigues. He also handed us a package of straight pins.

"It's important for the NVA to see the Airborne patch," he explained, pacing up and down, "to know that the men who wore them were hard to defeat."

Prior to this, the American soldiers had been using the ace of spades to mark the bodies of the enemy killed. We would receive full boxes of playing cards, every one of them an ace of spades, so we had plenty. But now our mission was to spread the eagle. For every enemy we killed, we were to mark them by taking a patch and pinning it to their body, ideally on the cheek. We were told that the Vietnamese had traditional beliefs about various parts of the human body and that they were very superstitious. They believed certain parts possessed varying degrees of worthiness, starting with the head, so we were to pin the patches there for greater impact.

"Doing this," Sergeant Ruper continued, "will let the VC and NVA know who was responsible for all the dead bodies we'll leave lying all over I-Corps."

South Vietnam was identified by four corps tactical zones during the Vietnam War for purposes of military operations. The four zones were I-Corps, II-Corps, III-Corps, and IV-Corps. I-Corps, where I was, was located in the northernmost part of South Vietnam, next to the DMZ (demilitarized zone) between the North and the South.

"You should know," he added, "that between February 4th and 8th, the 1st of the 502nd was credited for 250 NVA killed in action. We know this by body count."

Upon hearing that, the whole platoon broke out in applause.

Now that we had the sergeant's instructions for waging the psychological aspect of the battle, I was excited to use up my patches.

For a week, we swept areas then moved on to the next. After a few days, we would circle back to the same area to see our handiwork. I'd smile at the marked bodies lying there rotting, the eagle patch still visible on them, thinking of how Intelligence told us that the Vietnamese were also superstitious about touching the marked bodies, that if they did, they would endure the same fate.

I found myself requesting more patches every few days.

FEBRUARY 18, 1968
WE LEFT LZ JANE BY CHOPPER TO GO BACK TO THE FIELD. I WENT ON AMBUSH TONIGHT. I SAW THE VC SHOOT DOWN A CHOPPER. NO ONE GOT HURT BAD. WE GOT BEER AND SODA OUT OF THE CHOPPER.

The gunned-down chopper was great bait for the VC, but they didn't come to rummage through this one.

At times, as we were getting ready to head out for an ambush, a high-ranking officer would come out by chopper to give us a pep talk—similar to being in a locker room before the big game—to make sure we were ramped up and mentally focused to fight.

A typical talk before we were sent into a village would go something like this:

"Intelligence has informed us that the village is being op-

erated by the Viet Cong, and it's full of Viet Cong sympathizers. You're to go in for a search-and-destroy mission. Take the
rice, shoot the farm animals, kill everything that moves, burn
everything. There should be nothing left. If you don't do it
right today, you'll have to go back tomorrow and do it again."

He'd pause, then ask, "How many of you have little brothers back at home?"

As I'd slowly raise my hand, I'd look around to see several
other hands going up. My brother was only nine years old. In
fact, I had received a letter from him thanking me for the satin
coat I bought and sent home. My mom said he hadn't taken
the coat off and had been showing it off to anyone who would
listen. His thank-you letter included a picture of a 1968
Corvette he'd cut out of the newspaper.

"If you fail to do this job correctly," the officer would add,
"your brothers will have to come over and finish the job. You
got that? The gook we let get away today might be the one
who kills your little brother tomorrow."

The thought of my brother being here sickened me. Everything in me said I needed to protect him. I'd walk away from
those villages with the huts devoured by flames.

As we humped all afternoon toward the village, the rain
ceasing only briefly, thoughts about being bad at this job, going home in a body bag, and having my brother finish this for
us clouded my mind. It wasn't until we stopped for a break
that I was able to shift my thoughts to something else. A
pagoda, whose steps made fantastic seats, loomed in front of
us. We scrambled onto the steps to take a load off, not knowing how long the break would last. Stretching my legs, the guys
next to me started up a conversation.

"That M79 Thump gun you're dragging around," one of them said, "I'd hate to lug that thing. How the hell can it be effective if you have to put the thing together before you can even shoot?"

I looked down at it, at how it was broken down to carry it, looking like it was cut in half.

"Seriously, man," he continued, "you're too slow. How long would it take you to shoot if someone walked up on you?"

His words were starting to make my blood boil. What did they mean I was slow?

The razzing continued.

"Our M16s can be flicked on from the safety with lightning speed."

"I'm fast with it," I countered, defensive.

"Bullshit," said William Ballo, an African American from Detroit.

William and I had met at Fort Campbell and we got along easily. Had it not been for the lectures earlier in the day, I might not have cared what he said to me. But right then, I felt I had something to prove.

I looked straight at Ballo's face. "I know I'm faster than you."

He threw back his head and laughed. All of his perfectly straight white teeth gleamed against his dark skin.

"Come on," I said. "I'll show you."

We stood up back to back with the pagoda behind us, the steps filled with a captive audience. I had a grenade shell in the M79, and we marched off a few steps to separate from each other. We turned on our heels as if enacting a scene from an old Western.

Practice had enabled me to hold my weapon by the stock and with one arm flick the gun, causing the barrel to lock in place. In a split second, I could pop the safety with one finger and pull the trigger. Caught up in our movie-style standoff, out of habit, I pulled. I heard the thump and watched the grenade whiz right past Ballo's head. The look of shock on his face made me realize in an instant what had happened. I had been quicker than he was, yes. But had he been a bad guy, I would have missed and been dead.

Ballo looked up to the sky and moved his lips to thank God. In that moment, I didn't think about how I would have felt had I hit him. My only thought was that I needed better aim.

"Damn," I said laughing. "That was just like The Rifleman, eh Ballo?"

"Yeah," he said, still a bit stunned. "Just like him."

After that, we rejoined the others on the steps and the conversation drifted to other things. No hard feelings. That's how brothers do it.

CHAPTER
ELEVEN

POP SMOKE

SOON AFTER THE CLOSE call between Ballo and me, they handed out smoke grenades—two each for all of us except the RTO, who had to carry more.

"Here's the drill," Lt. Hale explained. "When we need choppers to come pick us up, the RTO will ignite a colored smoke grenade. The RTO will say the position is marked and what color it's marked with. The chopper pilot'll confirm the color when he sees it. Then, the RTO'll pop another one of a different color. The pilot will then confirm seeing the new color."

He went on to warn us that charlie also ignited smoke grenades, and if the choppers weren't diligent, they could end up in a trap.

"It's happened many times that the chopper pilot called out that he saw red smoke when the RTO had popped a purple grenade, or the pilot called the first color correctly but then the second color was wrong."

I saw some guys glance around, their eyes betraying that the last bit set some unease in us.

Once we understood how it would work, we did a practice run. The sulphur smell of the smoke hung in the air like a dense fog for some time, lingering in my nose and adhering to my sweat-covered fatigues. I didn't care, though. The smell would signify leaving a scene and being in a chopper, and that I loved.

FEBRUARY 20, 1968
WE SAT AROUND AND GUARDED THE BRIDGE ON HIGHWAY ONE TODAY. WE WENT ON AMBUSH TONIGHT. WE DIDN'T GET ANYTHING BUT WE WERE COLD AND WET.

The winter monsoon was beginning to hit, which meant the sweltering heat and warm rain were starting to fade. It wasn't cold, but it was colder than it had been. As I said, Vietnam seemed to have no weather that was desirable, but it was nice to get a break from the heat, if nothing else.

We were also getting braver. Jumping from the chopper all at once rocked it back and forth, making it more difficult for the pilot to hold the chopper steady—especially if he was less experienced. For this reason, the door gunners told us not to jump as a group. But on our next jump, hovering five feet from the ground in the chopper's slow attempt to land, we ignored the door gunners and decided to bail out. Surging with adrenaline, jumping without a second thought became the norm. Upon landing, we'd sprint to get to the wood line.

With the rain steady and relentless, our gear would be soaked, making it feel doubled in weight. I wondered how I could be humping, sitting, and lying in rain showers yet still be so dirty, muddy, and itchy. I felt like I was wet all the way to my bones.

That day, our mission took us to a village to check out and secure. Along the way, though I never heard anyone say "Stop" or "Break," we somehow knew we could pause. I threw off my rucksack immediately, providing instant relief. Then I pulled off my helmet and put my rifle down. Even if I only got five minutes, it was worth it every time.

I sat back and closed my eyes. Within thirty seconds, I thought maybe I was dreaming. I didn't feel rain and started to feel warmth. I opened my eyes to find a ray of sunshine breaking through the jungle growth and hitting my face. But as quickly as my moment of serenity came, it was shattered by a loud commotion. I heard guys yelling and shots ringing out. I grabbed my helmet and weapon, threw my rucksack on, and ran to the center of the action.

Glancing quickly around, I found a spider hole—a camouflaged one-man foxhole that was shoulder deep. Sometimes we'd uncover a communist crouching in those holes, all small and spider-like. I pushed my way in and saw a man, half in and half out of the hole. My focus went immediately to my tattoo on his arm.

Cantu liked going shirtless as much as possible. Shortly before I got there, he had plopped down and was peeling off his muddy, smelly fatigue top when he caught a bamboo bush move next to him. In a flash, he caught sight of a gook. The guy frantically pulled the bamboo lid to his spider hole back over him. Cantu grabbed a grenade and pulled the pin, then lifted the cover and threw it into the hole. He dove to the side and held his hands over his ears.

"There's a fucking gook in the hole!" he called out. Other soldiers moved in. "I was sitting right next to him!"

The grenade exploded, blowing debris all around. As it settled, Cantu crawled to the spider hole to check out his work and confirm the kill.

Just then, the sound of an AK-47 on full auto filled the air —the sound that had brought me to the scene. The rounds hit Cantu in the face, leaving only that tattoo to identify him.

Pulling him from the hole, we were all ready to fire. We had seen the VC so drugged that they were almost invincible, still firing their guns with half their bodies blown away, so we had to be cautious. Luckily, the VC soldier was dead. But so was Cantu.

I felt nausea rise up in me at seeing Cantu lifeless, but it didn't last as long as it used to.

Once again, I didn't have any tears.

```
Daily report.

21 Feb Battalion continued with operations and
had scattered light to moderate contact by
Bravo.

Results:

Friendly 1 KIA  1 WIA
Enemy: 4 NVA KIA (BC)

Cantu Florentino JR SP4 19 21-Feb-68 B CO
```

FEBRUARY 22, 1968
WE WENT BACK INTO THE VILLAGE TODAY. ABOUT 15 MEN WERE SHOT. I DON'T KNOW HOW MANY VC WE GOT. WE HAVE ONLY THREE MEN LEFT IN MY SQUAD OUT OF SEVEN.

FEBRUARY 23, 1968

ALL WE DID TODAY IS WALK IN THE RAIN LOOKING FOR VC I WENT ON AN AMBUSH TONIGHT. WE DIDN'T FIND ANYTHING IT WAS A LONG WET NIGHT.

FEBRUARY 24, 1968

WE WALKED TO THE BRIDGE FROM THE SAND FLATS TODAY (THE STREET WITHOUT JOY). WE JUST SAT AROUND THE FIRE AND TRIED TO KEEP WARM AND DRY. THIS RAIN IS REALLY MESSING US UP. IT HAS BEEN ABOUT A MONTH NOW AND IT HAS RAINED DAY AND NIGHT. EXCEPT FOR THAT MOMENT I FELT THE RAYS ON MY FACE, THE SUN HASN'T BEEN OUT THIS MONTH YET.

IF THE BOOT
FITS

FOR MOST OF 1968, the 2nd BDE/101st Airborne pulled security where the An Lo Bridge crossed the Song Bo River. The companies rotated between sweeping villages, doing ambushes, pulling bunker guard, and trying not to die.

One day, we got the day off and were able to go get haircuts. The GIs lined up and the Army paid the barber for each one. Getting a haircut in-country was like no other I'd ever had. For one, the clippers didn't use electricity, so the Vietnamese barber used his hands to make them work. His "cutting" hand would move so fast that it would almost blur. I couldn't take my eyes off it as I watched him give my brothers a smooth military cut, which was exactly what we needed.

After that, we explored the village and I found a rain suit for ten cents—money well spent for the monsoon season. I wanted the extra layer for the night rains, knowing our routine would resume that evening. I felt like a cop on patrol, making our rounds, going back to the same areas and looking for trouble, drawing out fire and hoping we didn't find it.

After sweeping the area and finding it clear, we found the highest ground to avoid sitting in puddles all night. The highest point was the cemetery. At one time, it would have given me the heebie-jeebies to take refuge there, but death was different now. We dug in for the night in a four-man position and decided to put our ponchos together to make a tent.

My problem was that one of the four guys was Dannucci. I had been avoiding that guy since we landed in-country. Back at Fort Campbell, on a night when Dannucci was drunk, we ended up in a fight. I don't even know what it was over; he was drunk and wild and ended up in jail. I didn't think I'd see him again, but sure enough—he got out of the slammer and headed over to Vietnam with us.

When we first got to Camp Evans, we ran into his brother, a Marine who was heading home. I don't know if it was a coincidence that Dannucci saw him or if the Army planned it that way, but all the guys in my company circled him, pumping him for information on what Vietnam was like and what he could tell us. I wanted to know too, but I didn't want to take my chances getting that close to Dannucci; after all, as far as I was concerned, he was still pissed off for reasons lost on me.

So that night at the cemetery, we laid one poncho on the ground and used two others to create a small pup tent. It had enough room for only one person, but we crammed three into it. The fourth guy was on guard and needed to use his poncho.

I didn't have guard first, so I was one of the lucky three with shelter. Huddled in the makeshift tent, the body heat warmed up the wetness, giving it the feel of drying out. Over time, as we made some small talk, the moisture did dissipate a bit.

In a four-man position, it was one hour on and three hours sleeping. Because I was the only one with a watch, we passed it around to whomever was doing guard. It was a high school graduation gift, so I hoped that no one would mess it up.

It felt weird to be in such tight quarters with the guys, but it felt good to get dry and feel warm. Leaning back on my elbows, I couldn't remember when I had my jungle boots off last. I knew it was at least thirty days. In a bold move to get more comfortable, I decided to pull them off. Peeling off my socks, I was mortified to see that my feet were so pruned they were starting to look deformed. They were actually taking on the shape of my boots. I thought a night out of those wet, muddy boots would fix that all up—and my comrades followed suit. We all moaned and sighed as we popped and cracked our toes in relief. Our tent smelled like nasty feet and ass, but it was home sweet home for the moment.

My sleep was deep during my three-hour respite and the dreams were vivid. Losing Means, a gook shooting at me and my gun not firing, Rita coming to Vietnam to take me home.

"Your turn, Stillman," I heard someone say, rousing me from the vision of my girl. Last on the rotation to pull guard, I rubbed the sleep from my eyes in the darkness and fumbled to get my boots on. I grabbed what I thought were my size eights, but I couldn't get them on my feet. I cussed under my breath, thinking I had someone else's boots. Not wanting to rustle around too much and wake the others, I decided to go without.

The rain had quit for a while, so I wrapped myself up burrito-style with my rifle nice and close—and dry. The night turned to dawn without any action.

In the early-morning light, I unwrapped myself to wake up the guys to get moving. But as I went to stand, the pain in my feet forced me back down to the ground. My feet were so swollen, it was hard to distinguish a foot shape at all. My toes were so pressed together, almost crossing over each other, making them look cartoonish. Even worse, they were a bluish-green hue.

I thought if I could get my boots back on and get my feet squished back into shape, the pain would go away. So, one hundred percent certain I had my pair of worn-out boots, I pushed and shoved my foot into the opening. No luck. Panic and anxiety started to set in as I continued to struggle, not understanding what was happening to my feet. The more I tried, the worse they got—and the more they hurt.

By then, my panic had roused my buddies and someone called the doc over.

"What'd you step on, brother?" he asked.

"Nothing," I stammered.

"Do you have any cuts or open wounds?"

I shook my head.

"Did something bite you?"

"I don't think so."

He squeezed my feet every which way. "Does this hurt?" he kept asking.

The truth was, besides some tingling, they were numb.

"Your feet are waterlogged, brother," the doc finally said. He turned to the RTO. "Tell the chopper that's going to be heading our way with supplies to bring the biggest boots they have at the firebase."

I was pissed. I kept thinking, *Why did I take my boots off? This never would have happened if I'd left them on.*

Sooner than I expected, the new boots arrived. I checked out the size: twelve/thirteen. *I'm in business*, I thought. I pulled back the tongue and loosened the laces. Toes first, I pushed my foot in. No luck. I tried the other foot. Same results.

"Can you get me bigger ones?" I asked the doc.

"Bigger ones?" he echoed with a snicker. "There are no bigger ones." He rubbed his chin and sighed. "We'll have to put you on the next chopper out, back to LZ Jane. The company's got to get moving. We can't have you holding them up."

And that was the start of a new chapter for me in Vietnam.

At LZ Jane, the doctor told me that the relentless rains had caused the flesh to shrivel and turn pasty, and that the mud and water that had seeped into our boots—and the friction of sand—had inflamed my feet. If that wasn't bad enough, the small cuts and tears in my flesh had allowed infection to develop. He told me recovery time was unknown but I had to stay off my feet as much as possible and keep them dry. To do that, I had to stay out of the field and remain at the firebase. I got to sleep on a cot in a tent, which was a welcome change, but it sure felt funny to me.

FEBRUARY 28, 1968
I STAYED AT LZ JANE TODAY. ABOUT ALL I DID WAS EAT AND SLEEP. AT NIGHT WE LISTENED TO THE RADIO. IT FEELS GOOD TO BE OUT OF THE FIELD.

FEBRUARY 29, 1968
TODAY I AGAIN STAYED AT LZ JANE AND SLEPT AND ATE. IT IS REALLY GREAT TO NOT BE OUT IN THE FIELD WALKING AROUND.

The next day, word came back to me that Boyer had been shot. The details were sketchy, but the important thing was that he was still alive. I had hoped he would be sent to Jane to heal and we'd go back to the field together, but he never showed up.

MARCH 1, 1968

THE SUN IS OUT AND IT IS WARM. I LEFT LZ JANE BY CHOPPER TO GO DOWN NEAR HUE. LZ JANE WAS IN A BAD LOCATION AND PROVED DIFFICULT FOR THE MILITARY TO GET SUPPLIES TO IT.

MARCH 2, 1968

IT RAINED TODAY BUT I WAS INSIDE A BUILDING BECAUSE I STILL CAN'T GO TO THE FIELD. I'M GLAD WE HAD A BUILDING TO STAY IN. ALL THIS RAIN HAS REALLY MESSED UP MY FEET, AND I STILL CAN'T PUT MY BOOTS ON. I DON'T KNOW WHEN I'LL BE ABLE TO GO OUT AGAIN.

SALLY

LZ SALLY WAS approximately seven and a half miles northwest of Hue, and 1.8 miles south-southeast of An Lo Bridge. Sally was a nice high, dry spot with nothing there. Railroad tracks ran through it and parallel to Highway One. We learned that the 1st Cavalry was the first US unit to establish position there; the camp would eventually be home to the headquarters of the 101st Airborne.

Construction started in earnest on February 28, 1968, with our guys tearing up the railroad tracks to use the material for bunkers. But when the Vietnamese found out we were ruining the railroad, they put a stop to it. Despite that blip in the plan, though, construction continued and I enjoyed helping with the setup of Sally. The light-duty tasks were things I liked, but my mind stayed in the field—more importantly, with the guys in the field.

MARCH 3, 1968
I STAYED BACK AGAIN TODAY. I DIDN'T GET ANY LETTERS.
I WISH I WOULD GET ONE FROM JERRY (BOYER) OR AT
LEAST FIND OUT HOW HE IS. I STILL HAVEN'T GOTTEN
RITA'S PACKAGE.

MARCH 4, 1968
TODAY I GOT A PACKAGE FROM HOME AND TWO
LETTERS. THE SUN CAME OUT AND IT IS NICE AND WARM.
IT FEELS LIKE A SPRING DAY.

Each day blended into the next at the firebase. We set up tents, built a bunker, and spent days off eating C-rations and talking with the other guys. I was also in charge of laundry. I'd haul all the clothes down there by myself, with a weapon in tow. A few times I got spooked thinking NVA were following me. When that happened, I wouldn't let them pass me, as if that kept me safer. Mostly, though, it was a lot of military traffic heading back and forth, dragging bags down to the Vietnamese women who were paid by the US military to wash our clothes. The water in the river was brown as dirt, but it was better than nothing.

With the nicer weather, I felt like being home more than ever. I still couldn't go out into the field and didn't know when I ever would again. But at least I got a bath a few times a week, albeit in the same dirty river as the laundry. When I first got out of the field, I hadn't had a bath for six weeks.

When the bunker was finished, they put me to work at the chopper pad, another light-duty job that consisted of driving the mule truck—a half-ton M274 platform utility truck—designed to hold a stretcher. I would pick up the dead and wounded from the chopper pad, then deliver the wounded to the medics and the dead to the morgue. The truck always had something on it: food, mail, ammo, bodies, etc. What I hauled in terms of supplies depended on what the guys in the field needed at the moment, and it often changed quickly. I could be hauling food when the call would come in that some unit had made contact, so the food would sit on the chopper pad and I'd have to load ammo instead.

When they didn't need ammo anymore, I'd load up the food. I finally understood why our warm food was always cold and our cold stuff was always warm. Sometimes the food never got sent at all. We were supposed to get one hot meal a day, but that rarely happened. We were lucky to get three C-rations a day, and even then, we only got one or two days' worth at a time. And those C-rations? They were left over from the Korean War. Salt was the main preservative for everything edible, and that didn't result in the best-tasting food. The peanut butter, for instance, was a joke. The oil had completely separated and you couldn't mix it back together. It was impossible to eat without chipping a tooth.

But since the C-rations were the only thing we could count on with regularity, we made do. Each package contained a plastic spoon, a four-pack of random brands of cigarettes, salt, pepper, sugar, non-dairy creamer, two pieces of candy-coated gum, twenty cardboard matches, and toilet paper that was wax-like and rolled up tight and small. Each one also included some sort of bread, biscuit, crackers, or pound cake. The guys before us demonstrated how heating the bread up with some jelly or cheese spread made it more edible. We would use our C-4 explosive—an off-white solid with a texture similar to modeling clay—by molding it into a ping-pong ball and igniting it. We tried to be sneaky by rotating who asked for the explosives next, but we got yelled at anyway; the sergeants said we were requesting too many of them. The fumes were terrible, and probably poisonous, but the warm bread was worth it. It went well with the fruit cocktail and pound cake, which were both platoon favorites.

We also learned right away to hang on to the can opener—known as a P38—that came with each package. Sometimes the P38 was missing, so we kept one hooked on our dog tags, just in case.

The thing about the C-rations was that they were pretty impractical in the field—they were packed in cans and were heavy, so we threw most of them away to ditch weight. We knew our first priority was ammo. You gave up food before you gave up ammo.

Besides losing out on food, tossing those cans presented another problem: all our trash had to be smashed and buried so that nothing could be left that the enemy could use. It wasn't until one of my chopper rides that I saw why the Army had us do that.

Landfills at the firebases seemed practical enough. The US military dug quarries to get rock for roads, then they filled those quarries with garbage. From the air, a landfill appeared to be covered in ants, which would have made sense. But it wasn't ants; it was Vietnamese people. Once the military left an area, natives filed in empty-handed and marched out loaded with stuff. Not long after it was dumped, people were there hauling it back out. While I was on light duty, I even witnessed that the pine boxes ammo came in were made into furniture and then sold back to the Army. Villagers also made clothes and handmade goods from our throwaways and sold them along Highway One.

We did everything we could to keep the natives out of those quarries. They may have been good guys just trying to help themselves by using our supplies, but we certainly didn't want to benefit the enemy. And in Vietnam, it wasn't always easy to tell who was who.

CHAPTER FOURTEEN

THE AIM

DURING OUR FIRST TWO months in-country, the 101st paratroopers had killed nearly 3,000 of the enemy. We spent the majority of our time finding charlie, capturing or killing them. We accomplished this well with the help of artillery and air strikes, which brought massive destruction within minutes. The captain would call in the coordinates when contact was heavy, and we'd always be the leader in the battle.

Except this time.

B company had been in the valley to the west of Firebase Lyon, hill 285, in heavy contact with the enemy. Our typical strategy was working until an error in adjustment of the 4.2 mortar fire caused the wrong aim.

Still on light duty, I was present when choppers flew in to LZ Sally. They dropped bundles marked with red hearts, signifying the 1st of the 502nd—my company. At first I thought they were supplies. But I quickly noticed that the items were blood-soaked, burnt, and shredded as if they had been through a wood chipper.

As a result of that miscalculated aim, twelve men from B company lost their lives. What remained was returned to us, like props from a macabre movie.

The final line of the daily report for March 26, 1968, stated that Retired General Cushman, 2d Bde Commander at the time, recalled it as the worst memory of his military career.

As it is in war, not much time is spent mourning the dead. Me, I continued helping out with whatever tasks they gave me. I cleaned M-16s, picked up beer for the company, had bunker guard. On April 4, I received letters from my sister Janet and from Jerry Boyer, my buddy who'd been shot. I was relieved to hear that he was resting in a Japanese hospital, waiting for when he was strong enough to fly home. He had been shot in the arm while on ambush February 27; the bullet had snapped the bone in two. He said he had only been a few feet from being hit by a mortar. "Bones won't heal in Vietnam," he wrote.

He wasn't the first person I'd heard say that.

APRIL 6, 1968
I MOVED TO CAMP EVANS TODAY. MY JOB IS TO WATCH THE RADIO. I HAVE IT PRETTY GOOD HERE. I DON'T HAVE TO PULL GUARD AND I HAVE A COT TO SLEEP ON. I TOOK A SHOWER TONIGHT FOR THE FIRST TIME IN OVER TWO MONTHS. THE LAST TIME WAS JAN. 26TH. IT REALLY FELT GOOD.

With the company on stand-down, my light-duty work was almost nonexistent. I spent the next several days sitting around, watching the radio, helping get stuff ready to be sent to the field. I also went back to LZ Sally by truck to pick up mail and supplies. I liked it at Evans. I was disappointed when we found out we were returning to Sally so soon.

APRIL 13, 1968
SPIKE [SERGEANT ALLEN] GOT B COMPANY TOGETHER TODAY AND TOLD THEM ABOUT THE NEW 60-DAY OPERATION WE WERE GOING ON. IT SOUNDS PRETTY BAD BUT TIME WILL ONLY TELL. IT LOOKS LIKE I WILL BE GOING TO THE FIELD PRETTY SOON. MY FEET STILL HURT BUT THEY SAY THEY NEED ME.

The following day, I left LZ Sally by chopper and was transported to the thick jungle of Ashau Valley. Luckily, I felt rested; I had become accustomed to the downtime and light duty, but luck was on my side: the transition back into the field was an easy one. The 1/502 Infantry had been released the day before from their mission of security at Camp Evans, and our job was now to climb a big hill and guard the firebase.

The next couple days, we had it pretty good. We mostly just sat around and pulled guard. I was actually able to get some sleep and write some letters. And on the second day, I even got hot chow for lunch. As I read another letter I received from Janet, I wished that the weeks to come could be half as good.

When I rejoined B Company, it wasn't the same. There were so many new faces that I felt like I was with the wrong platoon—the wrong company, even. Everyone thought I was a new guy. In response, I decided I didn't want to get to know any of the replacements. I figured they would be dead in a few days anyway.

During martial law we were instructed to shoot first, ask questions later. But from six a.m. to six p.m., our instructions were to ask questions first, then shoot only if necessary.

That evening, I saw an outline of a human, walking alone toward our position. I froze and slowly glanced side to side to make sure he was by himself. When he was fifteen to twenty feet away, I fired. Water splashed as he dropped to the ground.

I moved in to search his body. He had money of all types on him: coins and military script, American dollars, South and North Vietnamese notes. The paper money was folded as small and tight as possible, discreetly hidden on his body. This meant he could purchase whatever he needed no matter where he was located.

On his wrist he wore a watch made in Russia, which was highly unusual for a resident of the South. I reckoned he could have taken it from an American soldier or purchased it in North Vietnam, but the more likely explanation was that it was a gift from Ho Chi Minh. He also carried an American Zippo lighter and a 45-caliber pistol.

The most important thing I found on him, however, was paperwork commending him on jobs well done. He had gone north for training and was coming from Hanoi.

I had killed an officer of the VC, and I was ecstatic.

I stuffed the watch into my pocket, then I laid out all the items I found on him around the body and snapped a few pictures. Then I gathered all the items back up to be turned in to American Intelligence. I marked the body for it to lie there and rot, then returned to my two-man position.

BLOODSUCKERS

APRIL 21, 1968
WE MOVED DOWN OFF THE HILL TODAY SO WE COULD
BUILD SOME MORE BUNKERS. WE ALSO HAD TO PUT
SOME WIRE OUT FRONT OF THE BUNKERS TO KEEP THE
VC AND NVA OUT.

WE SPENT FOUR DAYS building and guarding the
bunkers we built. The Army knew we needed the downtime
because all the ambushes and sweeps had us exhausted, not to
mention all the new guys who weren't even acclimated to the
environment yet. As a bonus, we got hot chow and a Coke for
supper one night.

On April 26, we left the firebase and headed for the hills
—Ashau Valley. A jet crashed there about five days prior, and
we were going to try to find it. They told us we'd be gone for
six days. But by the next day, they called us back to the firebase
for bunker guard and to keep watch on the road as trucks
brought us supplies.

April 27, 1968

Well, last year at this time I was home on leave and everything was pretty nice. I thought the hardest part of the Army was over. Next year at this time I will be out. I'll be glad.

All day and night, the rain was relentless. The road was soupy mud, and standing water covered most every surface. Even if the trucks could start—which most of the time they couldn't with all the dampness—driving was next to impossible. Worst of all was that all the precipitation brought out the leeches. A four-mile walk could have us covered in hundreds of them. As soon as one would attach to me, I had to use my knife to break the seal to my skin and then flick the sucker away. When that didn't work, I used my Zippo lighter to quickly detach the leech with the flame. After doing that, the wound would bleed anywhere from a few hours to a few days, and the holes often ended up infected. Because our bodies never seemed to be dry, it was hard to tell if the moisture we felt was rain dripping or pus oozing. Mother Nature in the jungle was a tough opponent.

The green guys—or who we more often referred to as "the fucking new guys"—were clueless about how most things went in the combat zone. It wasn't their fault, but I had been used to my team, my platoon, my squad. The guys I trained with knew what to do, and these newbies seemed to mess stuff up more than they helped. Without my buddies, I quickly grew tired of being there. Plus, moving equipment and supplies by walking Highway One alongside the trucks was tedious.

To give us a brief break and help us cover ground, the guys in the rear would get picked up and moved to the front of the line. When it was finally time for our squad to hitch a ride, a truck was slowing to a stop next to us when one of the "wet behind the ears" guys said with a huff, "It's about time we got picked up."

I cringed as I heard those words. I could only hope no one important heard them.

Just then, the lieutenant yelled loud and clear. "Skip this squad, driver!"

That was all it took. Someone shoved the mouthy guy to the ground and not a single person helped him up. Completely pissed, guys started shouting: "You can carry our rucksacks, asshole!" and "Your next ride should be in a body bag!"

I thought for sure he'd never hear the end of it. But the bullying was suddenly drowned out by an explosion. The ground shook violently and we hit the pavement. It took us a minute to figure out that the truck that would have been our ride hit a land mine, blowing it up and propelling the men out, injuring all of them.

As we realized that would have been us, the putz turned into a hero.

"Damn. Your smart-ass comment saved us, man," someone said. Others echoed the gratitude. The shoves immediately became pats on the back for saving our squad. The jerk beamed from ear to ear as the holy-roller Baptist guy in the squad turned to me, taking the opportunity to preach to me. "Do you know Jesus?" he asked for the hundredth time, as if being Catholic wasn't good enough. I just rolled my eyes at him and walked faster.

MAY 3, 1968
WE STAYED IN THE FIREBASE TODAY AND PULLED
BUNKER GUARD. I TOOK A BATH AND GOT CLEAN
CLOTHES. IT RAINED AGAIN TODAY. WE ARE GOING UP
TO QUAN TRI IN A COUPLE OF DAYS.

The new fatigues we got were clean, yes, but they weren't new. And 90 percent of the time, they had someone else's name on them. I often wondered if the guys were still alive.

Some of our replacements who weren't Airborne immediately tore off the tab and patch of those fatigues. It ticked me off because it seemed disrespectful to me to do that, but like a good soldier, I kept my mouth shut.

RANCH HAND

MAY 4, 1968
WE MOVED FROM THE FIREBASE TO QUAN TRI BY
CHOPPER. B COMPANY AND FOUR OTHER COMPANIES
HAVE TWO BATTALIONS BOXED IN A VILLAGE. BEFORE
THIS IS ALL OVER, WE'RE GOING TO KILL A LOT OF NVA.

THE JUNGLE VEGETATION protected the village inhabitants, but it also shielded the enemy. We used the vegetation to our benefit, but oftentimes it did us more harm than good.

In an effort to defoliate the jungle to remove the enemy cover, the military imposed herbicidal warfare. Agent Orange was the chemical of choice, so named because the barrel had an orange stripe on it.

While planted outside the village in the early-morning hours, eating hot chow from our metal trays, the low-flying aircraft would spray the chemical over us in a thick mist, fogging up the area as we tried to shove the food into our mouths before it was contaminated. Frankly, though, we were all so

excited to have warm food that we didn't let the chemical fla-
voring stop us from eating—contamination be damned.

We never had any protection, and neither did the South
Vietnamese. They would spray at breakfast time from helicopters, or from C-123 aircraft fitted with sprayers and pump
systems with thousand-gallon tanks—or even from trucks, boats,
or backpack sprayers—and by lunchtime everything would be
brown and dying, like a fall day back home. By dinner, all the
leaves would be on the ground, the foliage killed within twelve
hours.

MAY 5, 1968
WE JUST SAT AROUND MOST OF THE DAY AND GUARDED
THE VILLAGE SO THE NVA WOULD NOT GET OUT. WE GOT
HOT CHOW, GOOD DRINKING WATER, MAIL, AND ONE
COKE. PRETTY GOOD.

Sometime that day, I was sitting with the rest of the guys
when I felt warm fluid run down my upper lip. My nose was
bleeding again. I figured I'd better talk to the doc. Blood from
my nose—as well as from my ass—might need some attention,
I reckoned.

"What's your problem, Stillman?" he asked.

"I'm having nosebleeds," I said. "And . . . uh, I'm bleeding
inside too."

His exhausted face changed to exasperated.

"Stillman," he said, "I have my hands full with the guys
who are bleeding on the outside. You just keep that blood on
the inside and you'll be fine."

I looked down for a moment then back at him. "Okay," I said, and dropped it.

I didn't feel sick, so I assumed the doc knew what was best —that it was nothing to worry over. I felt guilty for even bothering him with it. I decided to never bring it up again.

As the defoliant pushed the NVA and VC out of the jungle and into the villages, we shot them in their tracks. When we had the villages guarded, we'd call in air strikes. The Navy pilots would often tip their planes in such a way that I could see them in the cockpit. I'd always exchange a thumb up with them, recognizing a job well done. I also thanked God for their help.

After an attack, we would sweep the bombed villages, looking for survivors. Usually there weren't any, and if there were, they'd be history after we went through. Navigating the bodies scattered everywhere, we'd gather up their weapons and equipment and ready ourselves for the next one.

MAY 6, 1968
WE GOT ON CHOPPERS THIS MORNING AND WENT A LITTLE WAY NORTH. THE VILLAGE WE WENT TO HAD A LOT OF NVA. WE HAD AIR-STRIKES AND BOMBS ALL DAY. THE DAY WENT PRETTY FAST.

MAY 7, 1968
WE JUST SAT AROUND AND BOXED THE NVA IN THE VILLAGE WHILE THE BOMBS WERE COMING IN. WE KILLED 10 NVA ON AMBUSH TONIGHT. IT WORKED OUT PRETTY GOOD.

MAY 8, 1968

WE WERE BY THE RIVER MOST OF TODAY. WE GOT TO WASH UP AND GO SWIMMING WE ALSO GOT HOT CHOW, COKES, AND SOME CANDY. IT WAS ALSO A GOOD TIME TO GET SOME SLEEP.

MAY 9, 1968

WE SWEPT THROUGH A VILLAGE TODAY THAT WE HAD AN AIR STRIKE ON. WE DIDN'T FIND ANY VC BUT WE DID FIND SOME OF THEIR WEAPONS AND EQUIPMENT.

The Chieu Hoi, which loosely meant "open arms," was an initiative by the South Vietnamese to encourage defection by the Viet Cong—and those who supported them—to the side of the government during the war. Urged by means of a propaganda campaign, leaflets were dropped over enemy-controlled areas by aircraft, and incentives were offered to those who chose to cooperate. The Chieu Hoi program was considered marginally successful—and those who surrendered were often trained for integration into allied units in the same areas where they surrendered.

One night, while on patrol, the company had stopped to set up a non-defensive position, and it was my turn to stand guard first. The darkness and the quiet made it difficult to focus on anything other than closing my eyes; my head would drop sharply to my chest, jerking me awake. Taking deep breaths and shaking my head would revive me for a few moments, but before long, it was impossible to tell between real time and my dreams.

Suddenly, I felt someone shake me by the shoulders. I woke with a start to find three Vietnamese men standing over me. I quickly pointed my rifle at them, but they stopped me from firing by yelling and waving pamphlets in my direction.

They were Hoi Chanhs wanting to surrender.

Our captain told us that the defecting Viet Cong had walked around looking for someone who was awake—the entire company had been passed out from sheer exhaustion. When this information made its way back to headquarters, the battalion was immediately ordered to head to the beach on the China Sea for a short stand-down to help eliminate battle fatigue.

The fact that every one of us could have been killed that night did not escape me.

MAY 10, 1968

WE JUST SAT AROUND ALL DAY TODAY WAITING ON A CHOPPER TO TAKE US TO THE OCEAN. WE ARE GOING TO HAVE A DAY OFF. WE GOT TO THE OCEAN ABOUT 6:00 AND SET UP FOR THE NIGHT.

MAY 11, 1968

WE HAD THE DAY OFF TODAY. FIRST OF ALL, I SLEPT LATE, TILL ABOUT 7:00. THEN WE WENT SWIMMING. WE GOT HOT CHOW THREE TIMES TODAY. I WROTE A COUPLE OF LETTERS AND THEN TOOK IT EASY. WE GOT COKE TODAY TOO. WELL, HERE IT IS WITH ONE MORE WEEK GONE IN VIETNAM. IT ENDED PRETTY GOOD WITH US GETTING THE DAY OFF. I WISH THEY WOULD DO THAT MORE OFTEN.

———

Each week that passed, I would count myself as getting "shorter." When you first arrived in-country, you'd count how many days you had been there; when you reached the halfway point, you'd start counting how many days you had left. Psychologically, this was extremely helpful, especially since I was becoming increasingly annoyed at being fooled by people I thought were South Vietnamese. During the day they would help us, wanting to do things to earn money. We'd laugh and play with the children and give them candy. But come nightfall, we would find the same people, children included, setting booby traps and land mines, and placing punji sticks—sharpened bamboo stakes—into camouflaged holes in the ground.

"Wolves in sheep's clothing," I called them. I knew they had to be killed.

I feared the punji pits most because they were strategically placed in the path of US troops and were disguised by the nature around them. If a soldier stepped into one of these pits, he found it impossible to remove his leg without causing more damage. The other soldiers would stop to dig his leg out, but that would immobilize the unit, making us vulnerable. It wasn't uncommon for us to be ambushed while trying to free our friend.

If that wasn't bad enough, the stakes would be rubbed with toxic plants, frogs, or even feces, all designed to cause infection in the wound. In the worst cases, men would dive for cover and be impaled in the punji pits. Not even the Agent Orange helped to call them to our attention. They were virtually invisible.

It seemed that every moment you were still breathing was a miracle. Understandably, the newbies in the company, in my platoon, were constantly asking for advice, help, and information on how to stay alive. But I grew tired of it fast. It was a struggle to keep myself alive. By that point, there was no way I wanted to feel responsible for anyone else.

CHICKEN FEET
& PLOWS

ON TOP OF THE BARRAGE of questions and lack of experience the new guys had, I also felt that some of the replacements lacked the discipline the soldiers in my airlifts had. What's more, there seemed to be an increase in drug use around the firebases. I had zero interest in getting high—it was hard enough to be alert with the fatigue and the stealth of the enemy without an illegal substance making me an easier target.

I had also believed that the 101st was more disciplined than the regular army, and we prided ourselves in that. But lately, it wasn't the same. I thought maybe it was because people were being replaced so quickly, affecting the whole division. But it was a mentality too. The new guys would show up wearing medallions around their necks that looked like chicken feet—a circle with a line straight down, breaking off into three claws. The VC had referred to eagles as chickens because they didn't know any better. *Why would these guys be calling themselves chickens?* I wondered. It seemed dumb to me.

MAY 12, 1968
I LEFT THE FIELD BY CHOPPER TODAY AND WENT BACK
TO LZ SALLY. I THINK I RAISED ENOUGH HELL SO THEY
ARE GETTING ME A DIFFERENT JOB. IT WILL BE DOWN
SOUTH AROUND SAIGON AND BIEN HOA

Back at Sally, the new guys were easy to pick out. The dark green fatigues, the "on-alert" looks on their faces, the innocence. They looked incredibly young to me too.

Though some of the newbies could have been the poster child for the 101st Airborne, I for some reason couldn't bond with them. I focused more on the ones who seemed out of place. As I glanced down at my faded-out fatigues that didn't even have my last name on them, my attitude was shockingly casual. I thought about how I and the other seasoned soldiers were comfortable enough to take our shirts off between battles. These guys had a long way to go before they'd probably even consider it.

But despite the mixed company, I was excited to be back at Sally to inquire about my new job.

"The position will take you out of infantry," said the guy sitting behind the desk at headquarters. "It'll really be a peach of a job."

I was feeling giddy and moved to the edge of my seat.

"Switching positions might make you a door gunner," he continued. "You'd get to be on the choppers all the time. Might be risky, but nothing compared to what you're currently doing in the jungle."

Then he told me that the current position was for a driver.

I felt a tad disappointed but still willing. Then he added that switching would require me to stay an additional six months in Vietnam, which would equal eighteen months total. I was already six months in and didn't want to spend any more time there than I had to. Switching jobs would have been great, but the extra time in wouldn't have been worth it. I was ready to get back to the real world.

I declined the offer and got up to leave.

"You've survived this long," the guy said. "Clearly you know what you're doing."

I couldn't help but wonder if that was true, or if I was just getting lucky.

MAY 14, 1968
WE STARTED A REALLY GOOD THING TODAY. WE ARE GUARDING THE PLOWS AS WE GO FROM ONE VILLAGE TO THE NEXT. THEY ARE TEARING EVERYTHING DOWN SO THE VC AND NVA CAN'T HIDE IN THEM. IT IS A PRETTY GOOD JOB.

The Rome plows—named after Rome, Georgia, the city in which they were built—were large, armored bulldozers used in South Vietnam by the US Military's 169th Engineering battalion. Equipped with a sharp two-ton stinger blade, they cut down trees and cleared large areas of land, destroying enemy positions. After the trees were plowed down, they would be burned.

Our job was to guard the plow so that the operator could concentrate on the task at hand. It was also a great way to rotate the battalions so that we could have a break from combat. The areas around the plows were often quiet and free of fire-fights, which was a huge plus. After several days on that duty, I found myself reveling in how easy and fast the time went by.

I wished I could do low-key stuff like that for the next twenty-eight weeks.

CHAPTER EIGHTEEN

HIDDEN TREASURE

MAY 19, 1968

WELL, WE DID THE SAME THING AGAIN TODAY. THIS IS SO GOOD IT IS HARD TO BELIEVE. I HEARD WE ARE GOING TO HUE TO GUARD A BRIDGE WHEN WE GET DONE WITH THIS.

MAY 20, 1968

WE JUST SAT AROUND AND GUARDED THE PLOWS AGAIN TODAY. GOT TO TAKE A BATH IN THE RIVER, WHICH WAS PRETTY GOOD. WENT ON AMBUSH TONIGHT BUT DIDN'T GET ANYTHING.

THE TIME WE SPENT between guarding the plows and sweeping the villages had to be the easiest the company had ever had while in Vietnam. News of Delta company reported them doing road sweeps from An Lo to Evans with some light contact. Word had it that they discovered a mine, but before they could remove it, a civilian bus ran over it. They said no one was injured but the bus was heavily damaged.

Overall, we were all enjoying a relative reprieve from the

madness. And with things feeling calmer, it also felt like we were making progress in winning the war. We were certain it was only a matter of time before the enemy retreated.

MAY 22, 1968
WE WALKED OVER TO THE NEXT VILLAGE TODAY TO CHECK IT OUT. WE KILLED TWO NVA, WOUNDED ONE, AND CAPTURED FIVE. WE GOT A LOT OF EQUIPMENT FROM THEM.

As time went on, we saw less of the enemy. We didn't know if there were actually fewer of them or if they were becoming more evasive.

The 101st had the South Vietnamese Army attached to them, and their soldiers proved to be invaluable. Oftentimes the mere sight of a South Vietnamese soldier would force the sympathizers to surrender.

These men could also speak the language, including the slang, making them excellent at forcing the Viet Cong and North Vietnamese Army to talk. When we captured POWs, we would place empty sandbags over their heads and load them into the back of trucks, where they sat with their hands tied behind their backs. We'd sit down and enjoy a can of fruit cocktail while the South soldiers would go to work questioning them. We didn't know what was being said; many times we thought it was going well only to witness the South Vietnamese shoot and kill.

On one particular day, the captured weren't willing to open their mouths, so the ARVN—Army of the Republic of

Vietnam—had the RTO call in a chopper. When it landed, the South soldiers forced a couple VC onto it. I was wishing I had more cherries in my fruit can as I watched the helicopter go straight up until it was like a speck of pepper against the dark blue sky. Wondering what was happening, I squinted and saw a small object falling from the chopper.

It was a body. It hit the ground with a solid thud.

One lifeless comrade left to rot on the jungle floor was all it took. As the chopper slowly lowered to the ground, the remaining POWs suddenly had diarrhea of the mouth—and from the other end too.

It was psychological warfare at its finest.

CHAPTER NINETEEN

160 DAYS

WHEN THE MAIL ARRIVED the next morning, it was sur-
prising to get a letter from Coy. No one ever wrote the company
after they left wounded, but leave it to Coy—he told us how
he had healed, driving home the notion that he was indestructible. When I read that he was now at Fort Dix as an instructor
for new recruits, I couldn't contain my laughter. I felt sorry for
the training he'd be giving those poor kids. He went on to tell
us that he was depressed to not be in the field and encouraged
us to make him proud.

MAY 24, 1968
WE DID THE SAME OLD THING AGAIN TODAY. I WROTE A
COUPLE OF LETTERS AND THEN GOT SOME SLEEP. DIDN'T
GET ANY MAIL TODAY. THIS JOB IS TOO GOOD TO BELIEVE.

MAY 25, 1968
WE GUARDED THE PLOWS AGAIN TODAY. IT WAS A REAL
QUIET DAY. I GOT TO TAKE A BATH IN THE STREAM.
TONIGHT, D COMPANY GOT HIT BY THE NVA. THEY ARE
REAL CLOSE TO US.

WELL, ONE MORE WEEK IS OVER WITH AND I AM GETTING
SHORTER EVERY DAY. I HOPE WE KEEP THIS JOB FOR A
WHILE. I WISH I WOULD GET A LETTER FROM JERRY
[BOYER] SO I WOULD KNOW HIS ADDRESS.

During the last week of May, Delta made heavy contact. They returned fire and called in artillery, estimating the enemy element as an NVA company. When it was over, the daily report stated that the enemy had twenty wounded in action (WIA) and Delta had fourteen. It wasn't until we received a comprehensive report for 1st Battalion, 502d Airborne 101st —from December 19, 1967 to June 1, 1968—that we saw just how the numbers had added up:

```
Friendly: 59 KIA 393 WIA
Enemy : 852 KIA (determined by body count) 250
KIA (estimated) 129 WIA/POW
```

June started off with the feeling of making huge progress. We swept multiple villages, some days taking a literal ton of rice and a few VC, and other days a little bit of rice and a ton of VC. Mail was sketchy, as was hot chow, so we were hungry a lot of the time, but at least the days were going by fast. Our biggest problem was running into VC traps along the trails leading into some of the villages. Booby-trapped with dozens of grenades, these villages appeared to be protected more than others, perhaps because they contained valuables. In these cases, we had to be extra cautious in reaching and sweeping the villages, sometimes encountering light contact.

With certain members of the South Vietnamese Army—called Popular Force, or PF—alongside us, we had help blowing the booby traps in place. These guys were the lowest level of the SVA—villagers who volunteered for the PF and were guaranteed service in their home district in exchange for a lifetime enlistment (which lasted until age sixty-five, and the men could be deployed anywhere in the country). We were grateful to have them and regretted losing one when he stepped on a 105 mm booby trap.

At that point, we were collecting VC kills, along with their weapons—SKSs, M-16s, AK-47s—all the ammo to go with them, and their rice. Two of the newest captured VC were caught in a sampan hauling rice down the river, a method they confessed they used quite often. Sometimes we confiscated up to 10,000 pounds of rice in a single day.

The repeated stories from the Hoi Chanhs, when they surrendered, were that their leader had been killed by the Airborne. They were so willing to help NVA get captured that they would search out a US soldier to tell him about their guys who had fled to the mountains. Clearly, they were losing ground. One VC we killed was a messenger who had a document from his commander, stating that his men could not fight due to lack of food, weapons, and ammo.

JUNE 5, 1968
WE GOT ON CHOPPERS THIS MORNING AND WENT TO GUARD THE BRIDGE AT SIA CROSSING THE AN LO RIVER. THIS IS GOING TO BE LIKE AN R&R FOR US.

JUNE 6, 1968

WE SWEPT HIGHWAY ONE FOR MINES THIS MORNING,
WHICH ONLY TOOK A COUPLE OF HOURS. WHEN WE GOT
BACK WE WENT SWIMMING AND THEN JUST GOT SOME
REST, WHAT WE ALL NEEDED.

We worked quite a bit at the bridge. It was pretty hot, so building new bunkers was a drain on us, but it was much better than being in the field. On one of the days, a trailer truck filled with beer and Coke pulled up—we could buy as many cases as we wanted, so as you might imagine, some of the guys did a lot of drinking. Our other perk was swimming in the river to cool off after a hard day's work.

JUNE 14, 1968

WE ARE STILL AT THE BRIDGE BUT WE WENT WITH THE
PFs TO GO AND SWEEP A VILLAGE. WE GOT MORTARED
WHEN WE WERE OUT IN THE RICE PADDY. NO ONE GOT
HURT AND WE DIDN'T FIND ANY VC.

While contact was light for us, C company suffered heavy casualties during a sweep of a village that was heavily booby-trapped. To help them regroup, they decided to move them to An Lo Bridge. Once they arrived, they took over for us. We walked about two miles and set up for the night.

JUNE 15, 1968

HERE IT IS ONE MORE WEEK GONE AND I AM GETTING
SHORTER ALL THE TIME. I HAVE AROUND 160 DAYS

LEFT. THAT IS A LOT BETTER THAN WHAT I HAD IN
DECEMBER.

In our new location, the contact remained light and the enemy evasive. We rotated security between the companies, switching off from the bridge to the plows. While at the plows, we witnessed the Rome destroying meters of hedgerow, bunkers, and an entire village in a day's work, sometimes turning up bodies of VCs.

Two days in a row, almost in celebration of all the destruction we had facilitated, they choppered out coffee and cake to us. Nothing had tasted so good in a long while. We were able to rest and enjoy our treats before heading off to do another village sweep across the river.

JUNE 20, 1968
WE KILLED FIVE VCs TODAY. TWO OF THEM WERE GIRLS.
WE ALSO CAPTURED THREE YOUNG VC BOYS.
ONE OF THE KILLED WAS THE DISTRICT ECONOMIC CHIEF.
HEADQUARTERS ALWAYS LIKED THOSE REPORTS. OUR
OPERATIONS WERE JOINT WITH SVA AND PFs. THEY
WERE WORKING JUST AS HARD AS US, CAPTURING,
KILLING, AND SWEEPING THE VILLAGES CLEAN.

JUNE 21, 1968
WE SWEPT A SMALL VILLAGE TODAY AND FOUND ABOUT
THREE TONS OF RICE THE VC HAD HIDDEN
UNDERGROUND. WE BAGGED IT UP AND A CHOPPER
TOOK IT TO A VILLAGE FOR THE POOR PEOPLE.

JUNE 22, 1968

WE SWEPT A NEW VILLAGE TODAY AND JUST LIKE
YESTERDAY, WE FOUND A LOT OF RICE. WE CALLED IN
THE PFs AND THEY TOOK OVER FOR US. WE THEN LEFT
AND GOT HOT CHOW FOR THE DAY. I AM HAPPY TO SAY
THAT I HAVE ONE MORE WEEK OVER WITH. THE TIME IS
GOING BY PRETTY FAST. I WILL BE GLAD WHEN I CAN GO
ON R&R AND FINALLY CALL HOME.

At that point, we separated from the PFs to let them work
on their own. But while they were moving into position, they
were ambushed and later mortared, leaving six KIA and ten
WIA. Though they killed six VCs and captured their weapons,
the platoon leader was among those killed. Here they were,
both Vietnamese, but their ideals were as different as night
and day—and the North wasn't going down without a fight.
Even still, the Hoi Chanh's numbers were increasing daily.
They continually told the soldiers that they were giving up
because of the Rome plow and the Eagle flights. They also said
that the ones who didn't surrender were running to the mountains.

I smiled when I heard that. It meant we were being successful.

JUNE 26, 1968

WE HAD A LONG BUT GOOD DAY TODAY. WE GOT UP REAL
EARLY AND WENT TO THIS VILLAGE TO BLOCK IT OFF. WE
KILLED EIGHT VC AND TOOK THREE PRISONERS. WE
KILLED A VC BATTALION COMMANDER, WHICH WAS GOOD.

June 27, 1968
We stayed in the NDP today and got some rest.
We then moved over by the river and set up for
the day. We got ice cream for supper today. We
had three VC come to us and give up.

The next day, we were pulling security at An Lo Bridge when we saw something odd in the water. Rushing down, we hauled up twenty plastic bags that were floating down the river. When we ripped the first one open, we were shocked to find an NVA who had been killed in action. Each subsequent bag contained another NVA's body.

We had believed that we were winning, but our discovery confirmed to us that the enemy was, without a doubt, taking some major blows.

CHINA BEACH

THE TRANSITION FROM June to July was calm and rather uneventful for me. The battalion stayed busy with sweeps and chopper assaults, and Eagle flights rounded things out. I was able to write some letters, swim, get my hair cut. And even though I didn't have too many Cokes or beers with the other guys, I still had a good time. On the Fourth of July, however, we all reveled in the celebration with cold beer, ice cream, cold milk, and Kool-Aid.

The battalion continued operations with security of An Lo, mine sweeps, and the usual search and clears. An air strike was called on one of the Eagle flights, and even though the contact was light, three VC were KIA. We also discovered three bodies that had been buried—two VC and one NVA—that had apparently been killed by artillery. The booby traps were thick and making things treacherous if we let our guard down, but we were proud to recover fifteen tons of rice, the staple of sustenance for those we were fighting for.

On July 5, I left the field by chopper for LZ Sally, where I would hang out before heading to Da Nang for my R&R in-country. I hadn't forgotten that I was supposed to go with

Boyer on R&R to Australia, but I wasn't sure when I would get my out-of-country leave, or if they would still let me go as promised. As it was, my in-country leave had been delayed due to the number of lost men, the new guys coming in, and the busyness of the battalion.

Sally wasn't Australia by any means, but at least I got to sleep on a cot, and have a shower, cold beer, and hot chow, and that sure felt like R&R. I also didn't have to work at Sally, and I was able to swim quite a bit by going with the guys to get the laundry done. I even got to go into the village and have my own patches put onto my fatigues. It felt good to have them there again.

A few days later, I left LZ Sally by jeep to Phu Bia to get a C-130 that was going to Da Nang, which is eighty-five miles south of the DMZ. I wasn't able to check in to the R&R center until the 11th, so I purchased the vacation items I needed from the PX and was glad to make some friends at the USO, who allowed me to stay with them at their barracks. The building had been an old French hotel and resort, and it was ideally located at China Beach. I was in awe over the area. The cloudless sky was the brightest blue, and the air smelled salty and fresh, much different from the smells of the jungle. Being away from the field had me feeling relaxed already.

My new friends were Air Force—they had probably pulled a few air strikes for us. They were great guys and I settled easily into conversation with them. Their barracks were air-conditioned, which was a gift in itself; it had been months since my body temperature had been so cool. Everything looked clean, new, and untouched, and even the bedding had a fresh linen smell. On top of that, the food was delicious.

There was a time that I had planned on joining the Air

Force, and after seeing their base in California and now the converted hotel for their R&R, I slightly regretted my choice.

On July 11, I left the barracks and signed in at the Army R&R center. It wasn't near as nice as the Air Force's, but it was better than the jungle floor. It consisted of a big open bay, set up just like the barracks we had stayed in for training.

That first night, we were treated to a USO show. An Asian woman sang on stage, trying hard to look and sound American. I glanced around at the crowd to read their impression of the performance. It seemed like everyone was just happy to see a female in a short dress.

The mood was upbeat and friendly, so I wasn't surprised when the guy next to me asked to bum a smoke. We quickly fell into conversation.

As I handed him a cigarette, he said, "Yeah, it's a bummer not having any money. It's pretty tough to be on R&R without it."

I was only getting ten percent of my pay, but being out in the field without anything to buy had made it easy to save everything I received. Maybe it was because the Air Force guys were so nice and had helped me, or maybe it was something about taking care of your brother in combat, but I felt like helping this guy out. I also thought it would be nice to have a buddy while I was there.

I knew that all the lodging for R&R was free, as was the USO show. Food, however, was a different story. The guy hung out with me for the whole show, so when it ended I offered to buy him a burger. I didn't want to eat alone, and it's what friends do.

"Great, thanks!" he said, quickly accepting the offer.

Burgers and beers were both ten cents each, so forty cents ended our hunger pangs and quenched our thirst. Afterward, he suggested we go for a swim.

I had a small bag of stuff—about eight packs of smokes, a hundred dollars, and my camera—so I got a locker to hold my bag. I hooked the key to my dog tags and headed off to the ocean.

We spent the afternoon on the beach, chatting about all the things at home we missed, what we would do when we got home, what we wanted to buy. I talked about Rita; he talked about his girlfriend. He hadn't been in-country long, so he had much more time left than I did. We spent so much time in the water that our fingers and toes were pruned. I would have thought being wet was the last thing I wanted, but the ocean was refreshing.

Another USO show was getting ready to start, and I was ready to get dry. The guy agreed to see the second show with me, and being early, we were able to grab great seats. I was hopeful to see Bob Hope, but at that point I figured I'd enjoy whatever they had planned.

We hadn't been sitting very long when my new friend asked for more cigarettes. I pulled my pack from my pocket, which only had one left.

"I'll run to your locker for another pack," he volunteered. "You can stay and save our seats."

I handed him the locker key, reminded him which one it was, and kicked back waiting for my cigarettes to be delivered to me. He was gone longer than I expected; in fact, the show had already started by the time he returned. But I figured he had to take a bathroom break, so I didn't think too much of it when he showed up with my extra pack of smokes.

The show was great. It wasn't Bob Hope, but the band played the current hits and the singers danced to the beat of the music. The crowd was bigger than at the earlier show and everyone seemed to have fun.

After the show ended, I turned to my buddy. "All that swimming has me starved."

"Me too," he agreed.

"Let's stop at my locker. I need to grab my stuff and my money."

He nodded. "Sure."

When I arrived at the locker, the padlock was tight. I unlocked it and pulled out my bag. I took a quick glance for inventory and noticed the bag contained my camera and all my smokes, but my cash was gone. I reached in and stirred the contents around, thinking it must be buried. I flipped things around. Still no money.

I turned to my friend, who was people-watching in the other direction.

"Hey," I said, tapping his arm, "did you happen to grab my money when you came for the smokes?"

His face twisted into a puzzled look. "No, absolutely not." He paused, thinking. "Maybe you got robbed."

"But the lock wasn't broken," I said.

He shrugged. "Well, I didn't even see the money. I just grabbed the pack and hurried back so I wouldn't miss any of the show."

Beads of sweat formed on his forehead. I didn't want to believe it was possible for him to steal from me. A friend wouldn't do that. Maybe being in a hurry, I wondered if perhaps he didn't lock the padlock all the way.

"Well," I said, shaking my head. "Dinner's out of the question now."

"Wait," he jumped in. "I have money."

"What do you mean? You told me you didn't have any."

"Um," he stuttered, "a friend sent me a money gram this afternoon."

I squinted. That made no sense, but I went along with it.

When he pulled out the money to pay for our burgers, I instantly knew it was mine.

"It's so great to be able to pay you back and buy you a meal," he said. "I feel terrible about you getting robbed."

I said nothing. I was furious and wanted to kill him right there as we waited for our food. I knew I couldn't, but I wanted to. I was sick that he could do that to me and think I was stupid enough to buy his story. I tried to act as if nothing was wrong while I quietly planned my attack.

After the burgers were gone, I told him I was ready to crash.

"Yeah, me too," he said, tagging along to the R&R center.

I climbed into the top bunk, and he took the bottom bunk next to me. I folded my arm up and laid my head in the crook. Squinting, I watched him put my cash inside his boot, then stuff his socks inside on top of it. I lay there stewing over my money being there; everyone around me fell asleep, but my anger kept me from joining them. After a few hours, before it was dawn, I crept down from my bunk—mentally thanking all the training I'd had—and stealthily made my way to his boots. I slowly reached in and grabbed my money, then tiptoed to the bathroom.

Flipping on the light, I sank down onto the tile floor with my back against the cool wall. I dumped my cigarette pack out on the floor. Then I took each piece of paper money and meticulously rolled it small and tight. I slid each roll into the cigarette pack and filled the smokes back in around it. With a relieved exhale, I put the pack into my pocket and crawled back into bed. A sense of satisfaction fell over me as I drifted off to sleep.

In the early daylight hours, my slumber was interrupted by the thief's outburst.

"I've been robbed! What the fuck?!"

I sat up in my bunk. "Oh, great," I said with an air of sarcasm. "Now we're both in trouble. I guess I'm going back to the field. I can at least eat there for free."

The guy just stared at me. If he sensed I had reclaimed my cash, he didn't let on. All I knew was that I wanted to get as far away from him as possible—but not by going back to the field.

Instead, I went straight to where my honest new friends resided—at the Air Force barracks.

CHAPTER TWENTY-ONE

LONG WAY BACK

July 14, 1968
I LEFT THE AIR FORCE BARRACKS THIS MORNING AND TOOK A BUS TO THE AIRPORT. ON MY WAY BACK, I GOT SOME PICTURES OF HUE. I AM BACK AT LZ SALLY TONIGHT AND HAVE BUNKER GUARD. 139 DAYS.

BESIDES THE WHOLE robbery incident, R&R did exactly what it was supposed to do: for a few brief moments, I didn't think about combat or the deaths of my friends.

Once I got into Phu Bai, north of Da Nang, the only way to get back to Sally was by truck or chopper. I didn't see anyone to catch a ride with so I starting hitchhiking. I had stayed at R&R longer than I was supposed to, and I wasn't sure how much trouble I might be in for it.

The traffic crawling along Highway One was ninety percent military, and I finally caught a break when I saw a truck with 101st, 502nd markings. It was going so slow that I was able to jump onto the back of it as it was moving, then two guys pulled me over the tailgate. I thanked them and glanced around, not recognizing anyone. But that had been the story for months. There were too many replacements, and I didn't care to get to know any of them. So I leaned back to enjoy the ride, thankful that I didn't have to walk anymore. As the truck was rocking and bumping along, slowly putting me to sleep, I didn't even notice we made a turn in the opposite direction. My eyes were about closed when the guy next to me decided to strike up a conversation.

"How's your week been?"

"Great," I mumbled, not making eye contact.

He continued to talk. I half listened until the words "out of the field" brought me to attention.

"What did you just say?"

The guy gave me a funny look. "We're heading to Camp Eagle," he repeated.

Damn it! I thought. *It's the wrong direction.*

I hurled myself off the truck, cussing myself out for being stupid. I was really going to be late now. Even worse, curfew was six p.m., and that's when all the traffic stopped. I had no weapon with me, so if I couldn't hitch a ride, I figured I'd have to lie still in a ditch until morning.

Thank God I didn't walk far before another marked truck came rumbling down the road. I jumped onto the back again, only this time I wasn't going to make the same mistake.

"Where're you guys headed?" I asked.

"Sally," one of them said.

I let out a sigh of relief and climbed on board.

As we labored down the road, I prepared myself for a yelling at. But when I got to Sally, no one even noticed. *Geez*, I lamented. *I should have stayed longer.*

———

Back at LZ Sally, I pretty much just messed around and took it easy. Bunker guard, cold beers, KP duty. It wasn't as nice as R&R, but I did receive a care package—my sixteenth—and four letters, three from Rita and one from home.

As the days ticked by, there wasn't one mention of me staying too long on R&R. I couldn't help but wonder how long I could have stayed undetected.

LIGHTENING
THE LOAD

I SQUEEZED INTO THE chopper and found a spot among the food loaded up for the soldiers in the field. A short trip later, I was back with my company. It felt good to be back, but I wondered who was still there from my old squad, and what I had missed.

Even though there were a lot of new faces, it didn't take me long to get back into the swing of things. A couple chopper assaults, a few sweeps, and I was in the groove of the routine. I was feeling good about what we were getting accomplished. The guys who got their hometown newspapers said the news at home declared the war un-winnable, but they didn't know shit because they weren't here. From our side, we felt we just about had this thing wrapped up.

Near the end of July—with 133 days left—the choppers came in and brought full loads of C-rations, ammo, and medic supplies, more than I had ever seen at one time. I was sure it was a mistake and blamed the screw-up on there being too many fucking new guys. It seemed as if there were enough supplies to last the entire nineteen weeks I had left. In actuality, it was probably enough food for all of us for a week. I couldn't help but wonder if another company would be starving because we got all their C-rations.

The majority of us had spent a ton of time out in the jungle, and we had done countless humps, so we knew it was important to decrease the weight of our rucksacks. Those who weren't yet wise to that were going to get a quick lesson.

The squad leaders were off in a meeting—not that it mattered, as the Army never told us anything in advance—so we started sorting through the C-rations, picking out what we liked and considered the good stuff. It was like a swap meet. *Who wants the peanut butter? Anyone want to trade for fruit cocktail?* We packed enough for a couple of days into our rucksacks and shoved the disgusting items that wouldn't be eaten into a pile; there was no reason to carry stuff we couldn't stand.

After making our discard heap, we took our P38s and slightly opened each of the rejected items. Then, sitting by the four-foot-deep stream, we dumped them in to let the water ruin them. We knew we couldn't leave the food because a hungry VC or NVA would be more than happy to scarf down that rock-hard peanut butter, and hell if we would do anything to help the enemy. We knew the squad leaders would have a fit over the delivery of extra food, so we were pretty proud that we had it all discarded before any of the leaders came back.

Once they returned, however, we received an unexpected command.

"We're going to lay up in this village for about a week, men. We'll need to be as quiet as possible, not make a single noise. We must blend into the background. There'll be no movement at all."

We all cast furtive glances at each other while the squad leader explained that it was going to be like a stand-down in an abandoned village. "We have plenty of supplies," he assured us. "We won't have any choppers coming in at all. We won't be doing anything except waiting and watching."

I imagine we all had the same thought, that the peanut butter blocks were dissolving into the muddy river water as he spoke, along with everything else we ditched. But we were smart enough to not say a word. Suffering through the hunger would be better than the verbal beating. Plus, the truth was, I knew I could make it without food; it was not getting mail for a whole week that was weighing on me. Food may have kept our bodies going, but the letters and packages were what preserved our sanity. As the squad leader's voice faded, the only thing that gave me strength in that moment was imagining the pile of mail I'd be getting at the end of the week.

The first day was fairly uneventful. We sat around waiting to see if any VC would come along, but none did. The next day we did the same and ambushed fifteen VC. We had no idea when or if more would come along, so we continued to sit and wait, with nothing else to do except eat up our C-rations. Once the food was gone, all we could think about was our growling stomachs and not having anything to put into them.

The village had baby chickens running around—scrawny little things with very few feathers. They didn't look healthy and were the size of a small songbird. Because we mostly sat still, the chicks got used to us. As they roamed closer in their search for something to eat, it was easy for one of the soldiers to grab one.

Desperate for food, he snapped its neck and plucked the few feathers from its little body, then placed it over the fire. The smell of chicken cooking enticed more guys toward us. But the bird barely had enough meat to feed one man a minuscule portion. Pretty soon, other soldiers were chasing down the little snacks.

The squad leaders laughed at us, thinking we had stuffed ourselves with a week's worth of C-rations in only a couple of days. One said, "Hey, if it's just a hot meal you want, you'll get one at the end of the week."

That gave me something to look forward to. The days blended so much that if I didn't X out each one on the calendar in the back of my journal, I couldn't tell Wednesday from Sunday. Marking off the days also helped me to see how short I was getting, which was another reason to count down the days.

When the end of the week arrived, so did the choppers—with hot chow, more C-rations, and a laundry bag of mail on board. I wanted to make a beeline to the mail, but they were already handing out the hot meals. Each was packed in its typical olive-drab marmite, and as soon as we received the earthenware containers, we eagerly popped open the lids. But our excitement instantly morphed into disappointment. Our hot meal was not only liver and spinach, but both were the same green color as the marmite. Even worse, the can no longer held any heat. The nasty-looking meal was as cold as ice.

There were other cans in the delivery, so we rushed over to them, hoping for a better outcome. Those held ice cream at some point; now, the contents were melted. Drinking sweet milk was better than nothing, but as was typical, the temperature of everything was the opposite of what it should have been.

More than the disappointment of our ruined meal, I was bummed about the lack of mail. After a week, I was sure I'd have a stack of envelopes and packages, but there was nothing. It wasn't that people hadn't written letters to me; it was that they hadn't caught up to me yet. Also, I never seemed to get my envelopes in order. Oftentimes I'd read a letter and nothing made sense, then a few days later I would get the letter that had first explained everything. But I didn't care that it was a challenge—I just wanted mail, especially as I glanced around with envy at the guys who had a stack of letters and boxes around them.

> July 25, 1968
> Well, it was a pretty good day today. We just sat around in a village. We got hot chow and Cokes today. It was the first time in four days. We then made a CA [Chopper Assault] to our new A.O. [Area of Operation].

In our ARVN (PF) compound where we spent the night, we conducted joint operations with four platoons and captured numerous weapons. We killed several VC in action, one of whom was the C114 company commander. Later, the report would show that a female VC was killed as well, which was rare.

The female was a nurse. She would spend her day walking

through the village, acting as if she was South Vietnamese. She even showed appreciation to the GIs who were there to help. She thought she had us fooled, and she might have had we not been spying on her when she thought we were gone. Sitting in the darkness of the vegetation, we watched as she tended to the Viet Cong and the North Vietnamese Army who came into the village wounded. Once we realized she was nothing more than a dirty VC sympathizer, I didn't think twice about using my M79 to take her out. With her body laid crumpled in the tall grass, her hat knocked from her head, I snapped a picture. Some of the other guys took her photo too. It was a proud moment to take out someone offering medical help to the enemy. I smiled to myself knowing that more VC would die now without her around.

CHAPTER TWENTY-THREE

LAND MINE

NOW THAT THE VC WERE often in smaller groups, we had to navigate numerous booby traps. The NVA was making them from artillery rounds that hadn't exploded—the casing had a wax seal that they placed in a bamboo cylinder with a nail in the bottom. They would then enlist old men, women, and children to bury the devices such that only the wax top showed. When a GI, or anyone for that matter, stepped on it, the wax top pressed into the nail, blowing scrap metal into the soldier's foot, often exploding. These and other types of land mines became the leading cause of American casualties.

The other type of traps they set were to situate explosives into holes they dug that were about the size of a five-gallon bucket. They would cover the holes with the wax-coated cardboard the C-rations came in—which was exactly why we didn't want them getting stuff from the quarries where we dumped the garbage—then plaster over them, like fixing a hole in a wall. With an inch of dirt over the cover, no one could tell that it was anything other than the jungle floor.

With these detonations a constant threat, we had to

trudge cautiously under the thick jungle canopy and biting cold rain, staggered as a company so that if one person missed something, the next person would find it. On this particular day, I was walking slowly, scanning the area back and forth, when my foot sank slightly into the soggy soil. I squeezed my eyes shut and braced for the pain. When nothing happened immediately, I called out, "Booby traps!"

I looked around and saw everyone else frozen in place. I was careful not to flinch even the tiniest amount.

My mind was racing. I was almost done with this tour, so close to going home I could taste it. Yet there I was, imagining my life ending with a goddamn trap. If I didn't die, I would surely lose a body part. I would return home, but not the way I wanted to. Alive but disfigured was never part of the plan.

As my heart pounded, a mixture of sweat and rain ran down my face. Images flashed through my mind: my parents, my love, Rita, her smiling face. I felt hot tears fill my eyes—not in sadness, but in anger. Minutes felt like eternity as I stood frozen in time—perhaps the last minutes I would take in breaths, that I would still be me.

The engineers were behind the company with mine detectors, moving along one of the trails that was a main path, about five feet wide. The dirt was packed so hard, it was like concrete. The engineers had taken cover but were in shouting distance of me. I was all alone as I awaited word.

"Clear!" I finally heard them say. "Stillman, the area's secure. Lift your foot!"

I took a deep breath, trying to prepare for what could happen. I knew the explosion would be massive. I had seen it many times before. *You can do it*, I kept telling myself.

I'm not sure how long I stood there, but I finally got the nerve to slowly lift my foot.

Once I did, the engineers yelled for me to run. I sprinted in the opposite direction as they worked their way to where I'd been to check the area for more traps. After about thirty minutes, they announced they didn't find any, but that the mine I had stepped on was indeed fully functioning. The only reason it didn't discharge was because I was so scrawny by that time that I didn't have enough weight to push it down. The cardboard top had moved only millimeters, not enabling it to detonate.

There would be many land mines in Vietnam—before and after that one—but that's the one I would always remember. Some kid didn't set it properly, I supposed, and because of that —and only that—I still held hope of returning home in one piece.

Early the next morning, hunting for Viet Cong, we stumbled across two hunkered down in a bunker. Their faces were stoic as we yelled commands at them. When they didn't move, we brought the interpreter up front to ask questions. They both refused to talk. So, forced to make decisions for them, we quickly and unanimously decided which VC was the stronger of the two and shot him dead. The other one immediately started rambling in a high-pitched panic, spilling secrets.

The interpreter talked fast, trying to keep up as he relayed that a village about a mile north of where we were had boo coo Viet Cong staying in it. He finally paused to catch his breath while we hauled the loose-lips VC to a POW camp. Then we headed in the direction of the village. Whether the information was correct or not didn't matter. We'd be humping either way.

Once we reached the village, we took cover and observed. I counted around twenty VC, and by the way some of them were directing people, it appeared that a handful were officers.

Once everyone was in position, we descended on the village. During the sweep, a battle buddy to my left turned to tell me something. But instead of speaking, he lifted his rifle and fired full auto right next to my head. I didn't have time to react, to duck, to move at all as shots whizzed by my helmet. Too shocked to move, I heard a thump on the ground behind me. I slowly turned to see a dead VC lying directly behind me about twenty feet alway. Blood poured from his fatal head wound onto the M16 he had been holding.

For him to have an M16, it had to be stolen from a US soldier. It was an early model with a split barrel, a weapon GIs had a lot of complaints about.

I walked over and picked it up. It was set on full auto but it had jammed on the first shot. The chief complaint about the rifle had been a blessing for me. Had it not jammed, I would have been dead.

July 30, 1968
WE WERE A BLOCKING FORCE TODAY AROUND A VILLAGE BUT WE DIDN'T SEE ANY VC. ABOUT NOON WE WALKED TO THE RIVER BY LZ SALLY FOR A BREAK. WE GOT TO GO SWIMMING

July 31, 1968

We just sat around and took it easy today. I took a bath and then went swimming. We got clean clothes and hot chow for supper. We also got paid today. It was a good couple of days. My focus should have been that I survived two deadly attacks, but I thought the days were good because of the river water, fresh clothes, and hot chow.

August 1, 1968

We have our NDP set up on the river across from LZ Sally. We are going to stay here for a while and work in this area. One good thing about it is we can take a bath in the river.

August 2, 1968

We sat around the NDP for a while and then we went out and swept a village for VC. We found one in a bunker and killed him. We also got his weapon and equipment.

The villages had become a hiding place from the Eagle for the Viet Cong, but not for long. Day after day we entered the villages, coaxing VC out, taking back what they had stolen, then killing them. As we destroyed the villages, we eliminated the enemy's hiding places and protection. The charlies we found there had two choices: begin a whole new life or have their life end abruptly.

———

The jungle had cut me, bruised me. The glaring Asian sun burnt my pale skin and then slowly turned it a leathery tan. Physically, I looked different; mentally, I *was* different. One thing remained the same: the chopper rides still excited me.

And the violence? It became simply business as usual.

August 4, 1968
WE HAD THE DAY OFF AND WE GOT SOME SLEEP AND TIME TO DO WHATEVER WE WANTED. I TOOK A BATH AND THEN WENT SWIMMING FOR A WHILE BEFORE WE GOT HOT CHOW FOR SUPPER.

August 5, 1968
WE MOVED INTO A VILLAGE EARLY THIS MORNING AND CAUGHT SOME VC. WE TOOK ONE PRISONER AND KILLED THREE VC. WE BURNT THE HOUSE AND THEN MOVED BACK TO THE NDP FOR HOT CHOW.

August 6, 1968
WE SWEPT A VILLAGE TODAY AND BURNT ALL THE HOUSES DOWN. WE DIDN'T HAVE ANY LUCK TODAY ON FINDING VC. AFTER WE GOT DONE WITH THE VILLAGE WE WENT BACK AND GOT CHOW.

August 7, 1968
WE HAD A LONG HARD DAY TODAY. WE SWEPT ABOUT FIVE VILLAGES ALL ALONG THE RIVER. WE DIDN'T FIND

ANY VC, BUT IT RAINED AND I HAD TIME TO WRITE
SOME LETTERS.

Time was a commodity that had no price. Every free minute I had, I would write—often prioritizing writing letters over eating. And despite the unsettling nature of it that we had all seemed to stuff into a dark corner of ourselves, the routine of moving from village to village and launching attacks made the weeks go by fast. The days were hot and sweaty, but the ambushes and sweeps were successful and productive. Dead VCs and destroying the cleared-out villages so the enemy could no longer hide there—villages we would later help to rebuild for the South—made me feel like we were doing an excellent job at what we were sent to Vietnam to do.

CONFUSION
OR INSANITY

LEADERS WERE IMPORTANT in Vietnam. Platoon sergeants knew more than we did and we needed their leadership. Their commands could mean the difference between life and death.

Each captain's and sergeant's tour was for six months at a time. Sergeant Allen had just left, and the new sergeant wasn't too well liked—probably because this guy, with his shitty, arrogant attitude, was so different from Sergeant Allen. He had never been in combat, and he had zero experience in Vietnam. New guys were annoying; green leaders were intolerable.

I had been in-country for nine months. I knew the mistakes to avoid to keep myself alive, so I was hardened in my own way. I had every right to have a shittier attitude than his. I didn't know if this guy was simply gung-ho or just wanted to make a name for himself. Or maybe he was overexcited and hoping the soldiers would come around and befriend him. Whatever it was, I personally thought he was a special kind of stupid.

When the platoon stopped, he'd poke around, looking for

a spider hole, hoping to get some action. I grumbled a few times about how doing that would get us killed, but a lot of good it did. He kept doing it anyway. So I did my best to avoid his idiotic behavior. And it wasn't just me; everyone was talking about this moron and how he was going to get himself killed with a booby trap.

We all knew that shortcuts could cost a leg, or worse, a life. Being led into them by a leader was undeniably frustrating. The Vietnam jungle was nowhere to stick your head into an area you shouldn't, take a path without checking for booby traps, or simply be careless and unfocused.

As the days marched on, I felt disconnected, moving more like a robot than a soldier. I knew I should be hearing about my out-of-country R&R soon, so I tried to imagine how glorious it was going to be as we rode on tanks to go guard the plows, then switched to guard the bridge. I had to change gears quickly, though. Before I knew it, we'd be back sweeping a village, followed by an ambush. This pattern continued for days, blending into one—until August 20th.

We were accustomed to walking during the day to scout areas for nighttime ambushes. On this particular day, we left An Lo Bridge and walked the main trail along the river, at least three miles, passing the area where we planned to hunker down that night. To keep the enemy from potentially knowing our plan, we doubled back and casually checked out the area again, getting our bearings so that we could find it again in the dark. We could have run into the enemy by doing this, but luckily we didn't.

After returning to An Lo, the sergeant confirms where we're going that night and that we'll be in a three-man position, in a circular ambush. Each trio is assigned ahead of time because once we take off that night, there won't be any talking. Before heading out, we're able to get some rest. At dusk, we load up our equipment and gear, then pack up our rucksacks and hoist them onto our backs. The afternoon rest has me feeling fully charged as we start out on our hump.

Before long, we know we're walking into an active zone. Screaming and gunfire echo toward us as the VC/NVA kill innocent people in the villages. As it is, walking in the dark is scary; nighttime ambushes are the most terrifying tasks in Vietnam because we can easily be attacked on our way to the ambush. Sometimes we go out only to get called back in, then sent out into the dark a second time for twice the risk. Most of the time we stay all night, but not always. We hope for a full moon and a cloudless sky, which allows night vision to set in clearly for the duration until sunrise.

On this particular night, we avoid detection. When we reach our spot, we set up a perimeter in an open, dry rice paddy. We can't dig in; it is flat with no coverage, like a wide open football field, with nothing to protect us. The sergeant decides on our formation, and muscle memory takes over to situate it without much thought. The platoon sergeant is in the middle of our rounded-up wagons, with the RTO by his side, reminding me of something out of the Old West.

About three or four hours pass with no action whatsoever. It's quiet except for nature sounds; every so often the monkeys scream, a sound that no longer startles me. In the distance we hear gunfire; across the horizon, a gunship is flying.

We sit in groups of three, protecting the leader the enemy seeks to kill, taking turns sleeping while one stays on guard. When it's my turn to be awake, I can't help but think about the next mail delivery, my time left in the jungle. I wonder, too, if I'll remember how to rejoin the real world again.

Suddenly, I'm startled from my daydreams by the sound of a hand grenade and the firing of a fully automatic weapon. By the count, it's unloading a full magazine, twenty rounds at least. I immediately think it's someone in front, but in a split second realize it's coming from behind. Believing that someone's infiltrated the circle, I shoot the illumination round straight up to light up the area, not waiting for the usual instruction from the sergeant to do so. The illumination is the size of a hand grenade, creating daylight to see the enemy but also killing our night vision. Simultaneously, we take cover in case we're indeed in the presence of enemies. In the flash, we're able to see that there are none. I also see the sergeant just standing there, saying nothing, not taking charge. I assume he's being his usual idiot self, but I also sense he's in shock. The gunfire has ceased, but I can hear men screaming. A lump forms in my throat as I get closer to my platoon brothers. I don't know these men, these replacements I've refused to get to know personally. At that moment, I remain detached. I see that one guy is dead. But then my eyes shift toward the guys who are wounded: one is missing an arm, standing frozen in shock, expressionless; another is letting out the most primal screams I've ever heard, his body peppered with hot shrapnel, his face contorted in what is clearly unbearable pain. Several of us approach him to help, but he fights everyone off, throwing hard punches in his shock and confusion, believing we are gooks. For all we know, he is blinded too.

My eyes return to the GI missing an arm. He makes no sound; I'm not even sure he blinks. If he weren't standing, he'd be mistaken for dead.

The rest of us try to sort through the chaos, scanning for the enemy, determined to know which way the fucking VC went so we can fire back.

Soon, we hear chopper blades. The RTO must have called for a medevac the moment the shooting started. We are close to Sally so it didn't take long. As soon as it arrives, it illuminates the entire area. Right away, the wounded are loaded into the chopper. I look over and notice that the sergeant is just sitting still, mumbling. The chopper lifts off, leaving the dead man behind.

In the swirl of dust, the RTO approaches our group. His face is serious and he's slowly shaking his head. In the lowest possible whisper, he says, "Wanna know what happened?"

We all lean in.

"The sergeant fell fast asleep," he begins. "He was breathing heavy and kind of snoring, but restless. From the corner of my eye, I see him sit straight up, coffin-style, legs out in front of him. He fumbles around and locates his starlight scope . . . lifts it to his face. I chuckled because I could tell he was still drowsy. I'd taken my attention away from him to scan the area when I saw the grenade fly out past us. I dropped right away and saw the sergeant pick up his rifle. He starts firing, yelling how he's killing the fucking gooks."

We are all silent.

The bastard had killed his own men.

I knew I didn't feel safe with him. That incident was way too close; it could have been me riddled with his bullets. I also knew there was only one solution—and that was to kill him. I wasn't the only one who felt that way.

We dispersed a bit, all of us seething, but within seconds I saw my brothers make a circle. I hastened over to it.

"Let's vote," someone said. "Does he live or does he die? All in favor of taking him out, raise your palm."

Every palm faced forward, including mine.

We were all poised to raise our weapons when a spotlight blinded us. It was another chopper coming in for a landing.

"Nothing better happen to that sergeant," a voice over the radio blasted. "We're coming to get him."

We all shot looks at each other that said, *Shit.*

They loaded the sergeant quickly and the chopper flew away. I looked at the RTO, and he admitted that he informed base camp that a problem was brewing. Anger flooded over me. I didn't want him to get away with what he had done. I also knew that if he came back, we would kill him.

At that moment, though, my bigger fear was that we were in big trouble with the enemy. Our cover was blown, we were without a leader, and we had a dead GI lying in our perimeter. Our anxiety was off the charts. The jungle darkness around us felt creepy, and no one was talking to each other; any words uttered were to ourselves.

I wanted our dead brother sent home, so I attempted to rally the troops to get him wrapped up. The RTO called for the chopper but no one else moved. We needed six men to load him. "Come on," I urged. Two men stepped forward, and the three of us struggled to get him onto the poncho. He was heavy and so was the situation. I could hear the chopper getting closer.

"Come on, guys," I yelled. "We need more help!"

No one moved. The wind from the chopper stirred up the smells of warfare: gunpowder, blood, sweat, fear. The three of us struggled to load the nineteen-year-old soldier who had been with us since the end of February—a replacement who was no longer green.

Finally, I watched the chopper leave, but it was hard to follow in the darkness.

There were several hours left before daylight would break. We couldn't sleep because the position had been compromised, and we couldn't talk either. So we pulled the circle in even closer and waited.

The next morning, as soon as we had enough light, we headed back to An Lo Bridge. When we arrived, no one questioned us about the errant shooting; it was as if it never happened. I wanted to talk about it, but no one else did. Not one person asked about the wounded guys, the platoon sergeant, the guy who lost his life.

We had the day off—I ate hot chow, bathed in the river, and got some sleep before supper. But I couldn't shake what had happened. Craving some form of release, I wrote to the one person I always counted on to make me feel better.

DEAR RITA,

WELL, HONEY, HERE IT IS ABOUT THE END OF THE MONTH. THE TIME SEEMS TO BE GOING BY PRETTY GOOD, BUT I JUST CAN'T WAIT TO BE HOME AGAIN.

First of all I want to thank you very much for the picture you sent me. I think it really turned out good. All the guys are crazy about your long hair.

My mom told me that they got to see you for a little while before you had to start work. I was glad to hear that you were able to talk to them.

We are still at the small town of An Lo and Sia guarding the bridge. (An Lo is on one side of the river and Sia on the other.)

We had to go out on ambush last night and it really turned out to be a bad night. About 10PM our platoon sergeant said he saw VC in front of him so he shot them up. But they turned out to be our GIs he didn't know were there.

Well, he killed a guy and shot the other two up pretty badly. Boy, I couldn't sleep the rest of the night. What made me mad is no one wanted to help carry the guy that was killed to the chopper. So three of us did it by ourselves. It takes at least six guys to carry a dead man.

I should be going on R&R at the beginning of the month, and if I can work it out I am not going to come back out here. I hope being over here hasn't changed me too much. If I have, you will have to

HELP ME GET BACK LIKE I WAS BEFORE. I THINK JUST BEING WITH YOU AGAIN WOULD DO IT.

I LOOK AT YOUR PICTURE ALL THE TIME. WHENEVER WE SIT DOWN AND TAKE A BREAK, I GET IT OUT AND LOOK AT IT AND IT SEEMS TO HELP ME ALONG

RITA, I LOVE YOU SO MUCH THAT I DON'T KNOW WHAT I WOULD DO WITHOUT YOU.

LOVE,
JOHNNY

MOVING ON

I CONTINUED TO DO MY job: guarding the bridge, the plows, the people in the villages. Ambushes at night. Killing NVA. Capturing prisoners. Some days I was able to write letters and go for a swim. Some nights I got some decent shut-eye. But truth be told: there weren't days, or even weeks, in Vietnam; it was just one long, drawn-out year.

On September 13, we were doing our usual reconnaissance when one of the guys saw a VC run into a village. Rushing in, we found more scrambling to hide—we killed six and took eight prisoner; the rest had nowhere to go, so we called in for air strikes.

First thing the next morning, the plows showed up to level the place. The body count for dead Viet Cong jumped up to forty as the plows demolished the village and all of its bunkers. We confiscated numerous weapons and felt the enemy dwindle even further.

It had been a relatively easy and productive week. I felt like if my next eleven weeks went by like that one did with no one getting hurt, I would be happy. I wanted to go home and to finally be out of the field, and with these lighter weeks I felt like I could make it.

On September 18, the platoon sergeant told me to take the next truck out and head back to LZ Sally, with orders for me to be transferred to the 199th. I wasn't sure who was more confused, me or him. I didn't want to leave the 101st, but he said they wanted to mix the units because they didn't want the 101st to be all new guys. I was far from being a newbie, so that didn't make any sense to me, but I didn't have a choice. I was so short at that point; I couldn't believe I wasn't going to finish out my duty with the 101st. All this time, I had wanted out of the field, and now that I was getting it I didn't want it. I guess I felt a blow to my ego being a paratrooper going to a lousy leg unit.

The next day, I left Sally for Biên Hòa. I waited most of the day at Phu Bai for a C-130 and didn't arrive at Biên Hòa until about 7:00. The air was damp from the rain that had just stopped, and after grabbing a meal, I was able to get some sleep.

The following day, I had to get all my records and clearance to go to the 199th. The afternoon was pretty uneventful, which was a nice reprieve; later, a bunch of us enjoyed a movie and had a couple beers. As we sat back and shared stories, I thought about how eager I was to get my stuff the next morning—the winter coat, electric razor, and a few changes of clothes I brought with me to Vietnam. It had all been put into a duffle bag and locked up, awaiting my return.

When the time came to retrieve my bag, I was shocked to discover it wasn't there.

"Check the pile," the supply sergeant said.

"The pile?" I questioned.

"Yep. Back at the end of January, we were short on supplies." I flashed on how the end of January was for us in the field. He continued robotically without looking up, clearly having had to give this speech before. "The guys in the field needed fatigues, boots, socks, and underwear. So we had to cut open everyone's bags to dig around for what they needed. We threw everything else in a big heap."

My mouth dropped open a little.

He pointed nonchalantly. "Look through that pile for your bag and any other belongings."

I meandered over and found my jump boots, still in a bag. Thankfully, no one had taken them. I dug through the pile but didn't find much of anything. I chuckled to myself when I thought about how naïve I had been to bring an electric razor to the jungle. I never did find it.

> SEPTEMBER 21, 1968
> THIS HAS BEEN MY EASIEST WEEK IN VIETNAM. I AM JUST HOPING THESE NEXT COUPLE OF WEEKS TILL I GO HOME ARE HALF THIS GOOD. I WILL BE GLAD TO LEAVE THIS PLACE.

From Biên Hòa I was sent to Long Binh for more paperwork. Then they put me with the 5/12 D Company of the 199th—the Light Infantry Brigade nicknamed the "Redcatchers." The unit was formed at Fort Benning in 1966 and hastily moved to Sông Bé, Vietnam, in December of that year. I missed being with the 101st, but being with my new company at Camp Davey in Saigon proved to be a breeze. The 199th was assigned to guard all the different bridges around Saigon at night, along with bunkers at each end of the bridge and one underneath. The VC were known for swimming up to the bridge and applying charges to it to blow it up; eliminating a bridge in Saigon would be beneficial for the enemy. But with us positioned the way we were, the enemy couldn't even arrive by sampan undetected.

It was the easiest time I'd had in Vietnam, yet the other guys complained about it being rough and how they wanted to go home. I understood the wanting to go home part, but I couldn't help but think that they had no clue what a "hard time" in Nam was. In comparison to what I'd been through the past months, this assignment felt like in-country R&R. I prayed it would last until my days overseas were finally up—and that the one thing I wanted most would come to pass: that I wouldn't see another goddamn VC or NVA.

REDCATCHERS

DESPITE NOT WANTING TO leave my unit, I found my-self feeling happy with the 199th. I made a lot of new friends, and having no gooks shooting at me, and moving around a lot, made time go fast. I also had plenty of time for some much-needed rest.

Though I hadn't been to mass all year, I had done an awful lot of praying. I wouldn't have even known which days were Sundays without my journal to anchor me. So when one of my fellow 199th brothers asked me if I wanted to attend mass, I jumped at the chance.

We walked across Saigon to the other side of the city, where the old church resided. Out in the field, all I had seen was Buddhist pagodas, so the church was a welcome site that felt a bit like home with its faded white stone and red-tiled roof. It was startling to see that the tall steeple held a broken cross at the top—a sad souvenir of war—but it was comforting from the outside just the same.

When we stepped inside, we found it packed with South Vietnamese. The entire congregation turned and looked at us.

Dressed in our battle fatigues and carrying our M16 rifles, we weren't in the least discreet. I felt uncomfortable being gawked at, but they quickly turned their attention back to the altar. I realized then that we were an everyday sight for them.

When the priest came out, he was dressed in the same garb as all the other priests I had seen. If it wasn't for the different ethnicity, it was like being at home, only I wondered if I would know what to do since I couldn't understand Vietnamese. Once the mass started, though, I had to stifle a laugh. The service was in Latin; I indeed felt right at home. The prayers, rituals, words, and songs relaxed my soul for the first time in ten months.

Later that afternoon, we were told that we were heading out to the field the next day. I immediately felt the anxiety rush in and knew my rest time was over. With six more weeks to go, I couldn't help but wonder what was now in store for me.

Imagine my surprise when our next stop was a pineapple grove. I loved pineapple; my favorite dessert was pineapple upside-down cake (my mom made the best). In fact, I had dreamt of it being the first thing I ate when I got back to the real world.

I was quick to cut into a fresh pineapple. The juice ran down my arms and chin as I inhaled and savored it as if it was the first real food I'd had access to in months. It was so much better than all that canned fruit we had been eating, and I couldn't help but gorge myself. Pineapple can be tricky, but I got pretty good at picking the ripe ones. The time in the grove was quiet, so I passed the time stuffing myself on the fruit. You can probably guess what's coming: I ate so much that I not only made myself sick, but my mouth bled from the sores the acid caused. By the end of our time there, I couldn't wait to leave that grove—and I never wanted to see another pineapple again, not even in cake form.

My self-inflicted pineapple aversion aside, I loved my time in Saigon. The city had fascinated me when I first arrived in-country, and although the landscape was broken from the fighting earlier in the year, the place still bustled with commerce and business. Vendors of all kinds lined the streets selling fruits, vegetables, and homemade items. The most popular spots sold animals, from chickens to puppies. I'd always stop and let the pups lick my hands, a bit unsettled that they were pets to us, but food to the natives.

Those little pups reminded me of my dog, Frisco, I had rescued from the railroad when I worked there. He had run out in front of a car right before I left for Vietnam and was killed. My mom cried for days believing it was a sign of my fate to come.

On my way to R&R in late October, I met a guy on the plane who introduced himself as Chuck. It caught me off guard because no one ever used their first names, only the last. We struck up a conversation about where we were headed and I found out he was on his R&R too.

Right away, I was leery.

"Do you have enough money?" I asked.

I'm sure I caught him by surprise, but I didn't want to be robbed again.

"Sure!" he said with enthusiasm. "I've been saving up for this for months."

I relaxed a little as he went on to share that he was from a small town in Iowa and didn't want to explore Manila alone. I figured he was a good guy, and we were encouraged to buddy up, so I decided to hang out with him when we arrived in the Philippines. We studied our booklets that the military gave us, which listed all the places we could go. If it wasn't listed, we were urged to steer clear.

Once we arrived at our accommodations, which were similar to a nice American hotel, we had barely entered our first-floor room when we were approached by a man who introduced himself as Ricardo and told us he would drive us anywhere we wanted to go in Manila.

He swiveled on his heel. "That's my car," he said, pointing toward it and smiling proudly.

I took one look at the sparkling clean 1954 Chevy and right away I was game.

"Okay," I said. "But we'd like to get some sleep first. Are you willing to come back in a few hours?"

"Sure!" he said. "No problem."

We were doubtful that he'd actually return, but at the designated time, there he was.

We paid him a third of the money at the start and agreed that we'd pay another third halfway through, then the balance at the end. He was pleased as we climbed into his classic ride and set out for the city.

Chuck and I saw a bunch of sites and took dozens of pictures, relishing our freedom away from the jungles, land mines, and being on constant high alert for the enemy. It was also refreshing to witness someone take such pride in what he did, both in taking care of us and in how he kept his car. Every time we stopped, he would sweep the interior with a feather duster and broom while we took pictures. The car was always immaculate, and we almost felt like royalty riding around in it.

When we got back from sightseeing, we grabbed some dinner and then Ricardo drove us to a high-brow club called The Showcase. The club had cold beers and a hot band, and it was packed with GIs all having a great time, including us. Once we'd reached our limit, Ricardo was outside, ready to take us back to our room.

The next day, Ricardo's wife joined us on our outing around the city, knowing once again exactly where we'd want to take pictures. His wife was shy and quiet, but it was nice to have her along. We told Ricardo we wanted to buy some civilian clothes and asked for his help. He took us to an American-style haberdashery, told us to tell him—and only him—what we wanted, and that he would haggle for a bargain. So we picked out what we liked and handed him the stack. He negotiated a great deal for us, and we tipped him generously. Ricardo even took us to the WWII cemetery, where the soldiers were laid to rest instead of being sent home. It was a beautiful place, but it was even more sobering to be there in light of the two narrow escapes I'd managed only weeks before.

Over the next two days, I went swimming in the hotel pool, saw a movie, ate out at restaurants, and returned to the club each night. It wasn't cheap to go to the club, but it sure was fun. During those hours filled with drinking and music and everyone having a good time, I could almost forget that I had to return to Vietnam for my final weeks in the field.

October 31 marked the end of my R&R in Manila. After not much sleep, I dragged myself up at 4:00 a.m. to go back to Saigon. Chuck and I shared the room there, which had a small balcony where we could watch the sun set over the city. Leaning back in our chaises, we could see choppers and cracks of light from the gunners firing in the distance. As the city grew darker and quieted down, the battle sounds increased. It was like having a front row seat to a war movie—one we'd once again find ourselves players in within the inside of a week.

THIRTY DAYS

NOVEMBER 2, 1968
WELL, I WAS BACK AT LONG BINH TODAY. I HAD TO GET
MY STUFF READY TO GO TO THE FIELD, THEN THE TRUCK
TOOK ME AS FAR AS THE FIREBASE. I SAW TWO MOVIES
AND HAD SOME BEER THERE. SORRY TO SAY MY R&R IS
OVER. BACK TO THE FIELD FOR ABOUT THIRTY DAYS.
THEN I WILL GO HOME FOR MY BIG R&R FOREVER. I
WILL BE GLAD WHEN MY YEAR IS OVER.

NOVEMBER 3, 1968
TODAY I HAD TO STAY AT THE FIREBASE UNTIL ABOUT
6:00 BEFORE I COULD GET A RIDE OUT TO THE
COMPANY. I WROTE SOME LETTERS AND THEN GOT SOME
SLEEP. I GOT MY BIRTHDAY CAKE TODAY.

NOVEMBER 6, 1968
WE WALKED AROUND UNTIL ABOUT NOON LOOKING FOR
VC. THEN WE STOPPED FOR THE DAY TO SET AN LZ
FOR THE RESUPPLY. IT WAS A PRETTY EASY DAY. WHAT
A WAY TO SPEND A BIRTHDAY!

THE TIME BACK WITH THE 199th really gave me the feeling of things winding down. We did a couple operations where we were choppered out to look for VC—I still got a rush from being on those birds—but we never did see any VC or NVA and I didn't even fire my weapon. Other than that, we had a battalion party at the firebase, got free beer, Cokes, and food, and we had bands that played all day one of the days. I was both shocked and relieved that the 199th didn't do anything compared to the 101st.

On November 17, we moved to the city limits of Saigon, and I found out that I got a seven-day drop, which meant that my date to go home was moved up seven days. I was also told that I wouldn't have to go out on any more operations. Being at the tale end of my time in Vietnam, I could see a light at the end of my tunnel called the real world.

Once you had less time left than what you'd spent, it was called being short; once you were counting down the final month like I was, it was called being "too short." When you reached that point, fellow soldiers and the ranks above you gave you different treatment. The feat of being too short was a huge accomplishment.

I had so much time to write letters that I actually got tired of writing them. I had time to explore and I wanted to take advantage of it, so I went to a parade on the firebase, spent time at the USO, finished reading a book, and even took a steam bath. I had never felt so clean in my life. I decided right then and there that when I got married and had a house, I was going to put a steam bath in the basement.

That week of doing exactly what I wanted to do and no more was the best week I'd spent overseas. I had so much freedom that if the company went on ambush, I could go if I felt like it; otherwise, I just stayed back. They even asked me to teach a few classes on things a person needed to know when in Vietnam. It was precisely the kind of class I could have used when I arrived.

On December 1, I received my orders to go home. I cleaned and organized everything a little each day, and by December 5, I was at the airport in Saigon ready to take a civilian plane back to the States. I didn't get my seven-day drop like they told me; I actually waited longer to get a flight because of guys going home for Christmas. If you signed up for an additional six months in Nam, you got a thirty-day trip home for the holidays.

When they finally called my name, instead of getting a flight, they wanted to send me back up north to Cam Ranh Bay because they thought I would have a better chance of a flight from there.

"Don't worry about the wings on the C-130," the guy says to me, serious as a heart attack. "They've been falling off, but we think we have a good one."

I gave him a fake half chuckle. His lame attempt at a joke only pissed me off. No soldier wanted to imagine, even in jest, that he made it all the way through a year in Vietnam to die on an inferior plane on his way home.

As I sat on the tarmac at Cam Ranh Bay, I scanned the area, thinking there would be a lot of soldiers there from the

101st. I was eager to catch up with them; if I was lucky, some of my company would be on the same flight. I thought it was only right that we had come together and we'd leave together. Just then, I saw a guy run past me with the familiar eagle patch.

"Ramos!" I called out.

He turned. "Oh, hey Stillman!"

"Where is everyone?" I asked.

He shrugged. "We're it."

I couldn't believe it. Out of the thousands who had been shipped over with me, there was only one going back on my flight. I thought about joining Ramos but didn't. If I had, I later discovered, I would have seen a handful of other guys from my unit going home. Instead, I stayed planted where I was, feeling proud in my summer dress uniform and tightly clutching the Chinese carbine I had obtained on one of the ambushes up north. It had a twelve-inch bayonet that was folded back neatly, and it was placed in a vinyl sleeve for protection. The MPs put up a hard fight about me taking that enemy rifle home. What should have been a simple piece of paper turned into a three-day wait period—and me getting more and more frustrated.

Once on the plane, I leaned the rifle up against the airplane wall and laid my head against it as I looked out the window. As the plane began its taxi, the flight attendants, who were all older than we were, made their way through the cabin asking if any of the men needed anything. The GIs were flirty with them, making the attendants giggle. They were happy to give us whatever we asked for: a Coke, a comic book, a girlie magazine.

At the massive, brightly lit Tokyo airport, we made a quick stop for fuel. For some reason, as the plane took off, I felt butterflies in my stomach. I wasn't sure if it was from takeoff or the idea of getting back to the real world. As much as I couldn't wait to return to the US, it made me feel nervous too.

Our next stop was Fort Lewis, Washington, where I was surprised to find out that I had less than ninety days left with the Army. Since I had no plans to renew, I was told that they didn't want to issue new uniforms and move me to a post. I had hoped I'd get some leave to go home, but I didn't expect I'd be discharged after a one-night stay.

I had the opportunity to take a shower, but I didn't think I needed one. The truth was, I didn't want to leave that rifle. The Army had my dress greens cleaned and all the ribbons and patches sewn onto them for me. Once dressed, I was cleared. No debriefing. Nobody talked to me about my time in Vietnam. No one told me how to be a civilian again. They asked me if I was okay and I said yes. I didn't talk about the blood I was shitting, or how my feet hurt all the time.

I shared a cab with three other guys to the airport. I was excited that we got there early, but we had to wait for hours. When I called home to tell my folks that I'd be at Lambert the next morning, my sister Janet answered the phone.

"You're coming home?" she squealed.

"Yep," I said.

"Okay . . . Mom and Dad are at the American Legion hall. I'll call and tell them." She could hardly contain her excitement.

After the brief call, they loaded me onto a plane for St. Louis. I thought about the homecoming party I had planned over and over in my head—and how it was the last thing I wanted now. Suddenly, the guy next to me started blubbering.

"I've wasted my whole life in the military. I'm finally retiring and I've got nothing." His breath reeked of alcohol, making me wince. "You going home?" he asked.

I nodded.

He pointed a finger into my jacket. "You've got it made," he slurred through his tears. "You've got everything ahead of you."

I nodded awkwardly, unsure of what to say. Most guys were proud of their military careers. This guy seemed to think he'd thrown his entire life away. The next couple hours were long ones to St. Louis.

When the plane finally touched down and we filed out, the frosty air hit my face hard. As I let out a slow sigh, my breath became a foggy mist. It had been a long time since that had happened. In the near distance, bundled-up people on the tarmac bounced and craned their necks. There were scores of eager faces, but my eyes immediately zeroed in on my family—my parents, brother, two sisters, and Rita were all waiting for me. My frozen face melted into a huge smile. My folks had aged, my siblings had grown, and Rita had become more beautiful. I should have been elated, and I was, but something inside felt off. I had imagined that simply seeing them would instantly return me to my old self, but disappointment set in quickly as I realized how messed up I felt. As everyone welcomed me home, their words floated through me in a haze. I smiled. I shook hands and hugged and kissed them. But it was as if I wasn't really there, like it was an illusion or a dream. The weight I felt only got heavier; it didn't magically disappear like I thought it would.

The ride home was a blur, and I felt on edge the entire ride. Once home, my mom headed into the kitchen to make lunch, and everyone else went into the living room. My dad and I were suddenly alone.

"Need to talk?" he asked.

Inside, I wanted to tell him everything that had happened, but I had a difficult time staying in the moment. I couldn't relax. Staying focused on a conversation seemed impossible.

"Nope," I said.

Dad patted my shoulder. "All right, then."

I looked toward the floor, then stepped aside him and went down the hallway to my room. As I dropped my duffel bag, I noticed that Mom had freshened the room up. The bed was turned down with clean sheets and an extra blanket, and I plopped onto it. I clasped my hands behind my head and took in a breath, waiting for the relief of knowing I was home to wash over me.

It never came.

I swung my legs off the bed, grabbed the extra blanket, and lay down on the floor. I pulled the blanket up to my chin and fell fast asleep. Every few hours I would wake, unsure of where I was, fearful that my unit had been killed and I was left alone.

Every night that I was in the jungle, I would smell the earthy smell, the dampness of the monsoon. I would feel the insects crawling on me. The darkness would trick my brain into seeing jungle vines wrapping around me. I would blink rapidly and think I saw a gook standing over me. When I did sleep, the screams of the monkeys would startle me awake.

Now, back at home, my dreams echoed the same sounds, reflected the same frightening images. Night after night, I would wake to find myself belly crawling across the floor, reaching for my rifle, scrambling to find my helmet, struggling to breathe with my heart racing.

Each morning, I would greet my family and pretend none of this had happened.

No one knew I was still fighting a war.

CHAPTER TWENTY-EIGHT

WARRIOR TO CIVILIAN

JUST TWO DAYS AFTER I re-entered life as a civilian, our house was buzzing with party preparations. My folks wanted to host a celebration that I had made it back alive—my own personal welcome home. The Christmas tree was fully decorated, standing tall and lit in front of the living room picture window, and my sisters had records spread out, the turntable spinning over and over again playing "When Johnny Comes Marching Home." As they danced and twirled around the living room, delicious scents floated throughout the house, making my stomach rumble. The roast was cooking in the oven, Mom was mashing potatoes, and Dad was stirring the thick, rich gravy.

As I sat in the living room and watched my parents in the kitchen preparing this sumptuous meal, the likes of which I hadn't tasted in a year, my younger brother raced by me wearing the black satin coat I had sent him from Vietnam. He had beads of sweat on his forehead because the house was way too warm to be wearing it, but I was touched to see him in it just the same.

Once she had finished with the potatoes, Mom began putting together the pineapple upside-down cake that had always been my favorite. Upon seeing the pineapple rings, my stomach turned. I could feel my mouth burn and the sides of my throat tingle. I didn't have the heart to tell her I had all but ruined my desire for pineapple ever again.

Soon, guests started arriving, and the noise level in the house quickly increased. One by one, or in small groups, people kept approaching me. Truth be told, I wanted to be left alone, but I politely responded to their repeated comments and questions.

"I bet you're happy to be home." *I am.*

"Is it too cold for you here?" *No, it's fine.*

"Was it hot in Vietnam?" *Very.*

"Did you see Bob Hope?" *No.*

"How much rain do they get?" *A lot.*

Once I'd satisfied the guests' curiosities, I became a shadow at my own party—always keeping my back to the wall, scanning the room, watching for the enemy. The crowd ate, drank, and chattered while Christmas music played and the kids ran around giggling. Me, I faked a smile and nursed the beer in my hand.

I was happy to be out of Vietnam, happy to be alive, but I kept wishing I would feel like I used to feel—normal. I truly wondered if that would ever be possible again.

After a while, the doorbell rang. All the invited guests were in our house, and I saw my folks glance at each other, wondering who it could be. When my dad opened the door, an Army officer was standing on the porch with a briefcase in one hand and papers in another.

"I apologize for interrupting," he said politely, seeing the gathering over Dad's shoulder. "I see there's a party going on."

I swallowed the lump in my throat and felt my stomach flip. I didn't recognize the man, and I couldn't figure out why he was at my party.

"That's all right," Dad said. "It's cold out. Please come in."

When the uniformed man stepped through the doorway, the party went completely quiet.

"I'm here for Specialist Stillman, John Stillman," he said.

"That's my son," Dad said, pointing in my direction.

All I could think was, *What did I do wrong?*

I slowly stood. My legs felt weighted as I zeroed directly in on the officer.

He looked at his paperwork. "I have orders for Specialist Stillman to report to Waco Texas by December 17, 1968, for an airlift to Vietnam."

My heart started pounding. I found it difficult to breathe and my knees felt like they wanted to buckle beneath me.

Rita gasped and began to cry.

"I'm sorry, soldier," he said, "but these are the orders."

I couldn't believe that I had to go back. I wanted to tackle him, to crush the life from him, to squeeze his neck until his eyes popped out.

As I was visualizing his death, my dad asked him to join the party. "Stay and have a drink," he said cordially, as if nothing about this guy's visit was upsetting.

I lost it. I walked over to my dad, feeling the blood rush to my face. "Get that son of a bitch out of the house," I said through clenched teeth. "The party's over. Everyone needs to leave."

A silence fell over the crowd, and then my dad burst out laughing.

"It's a joke, Johnny," he said, slapping me on the back.

I knew I'd gone crazy at that point. Just when I was about to push the officer out the door onto his ass, he started laughing too.

"It was all a joke," he blurted between guffaws, "just a joke."

Everyone else then joined in the laughter—everyone but me.

"Come on, Johnny," Dad said, trying to make light of it. "This is my friend, Robert McNamara. The papers are fake, son. It was Robert's idea."

I looked at Robert, seething. *Another lame attempt at a joke*, I thought. All he had done with his "joke" was royally piss me off.

Rita's mom saw the look on my face and walked straight up to my dad. She looked him hard in the eyes and then kicked him in the shin. I could tell it hurt and it made my dad mad.

"All right, all right," he said, "let's not go crazy here. It was all in fun."

In fun? I thought. *He has no fucking idea how NOT funny that was.*

Trying to shift from the awkward moment, someone put a new record on the turntable. Within seconds, the party continued, but I was finished. I felt not only emotionally sick but physically sick too.

A few weeks later, I checked myself into John Cochran Veterans Hospital. The jungle rot on my feet had worsened and the blood I was passing in Vietnam continued. They put me into quarantine, a reminder that I was an outsider. I would feel that way for many years to come.

THE EFFECTS

EIGHTEEN YEARS AFTER coming home, the movie *Platoon* came out. By then, Rita and I had been married and blessed with children for nearly two decades. I loved my family dearly, but year after year, the battle continued to rage in me; controlling the anger took daily work. Up to that point, I had avoided seeing all war movies, but the previews for *Platoon* matched the images that flashed repeatedly through my dreams. I told Rita I wanted to see it.

The theater was dark and the smell of buttery popcorn filled the air. Rita leaned her shoulder against mine and I felt her love as the movie began.

Almost immediately, I tensed up. The realistic images, the sounds of the jungle war amplified by the theater's surround sound, took me back in time. The actors' faces turned into the faces of my brothers, the men I fought with side by side. When the GIs on the screen started killing the gooks, Rita had to stop me from clapping. Mentally, I was catapulted into that war, reliving my own personal story.

In the midst of the chaos, I leaned over and asked her, "How are they getting that smell into the theater?"

She looked confused. "What smell?"

All I could smell was gunpowder and blood.

Now, fifty years later, the memories are still just as vivid. Certain images trigger smells, and certain smells trigger images. In five decades, that hasn't faded.

I was home a long time before I was actually home.

Vietnam has never ceased to haunt me every day, to await me every night.

I still sometimes wonder if I ever truly came home.

AFTERWORD

In all the years of my life, I had never seen my father cry. But as the memories he had buried for nearly fifty years began to emerge in layers, the man who told me he knew no one's name on the Vietnam Memorial wall wept as he talked about the friends he lost, particularly the loss of his good friend, Ronnie Means. His tears were undeniably painful for both of us, and there were times I worried that as he faced his war demons, he would get worse instead of healing. I was treading on wounds I knew were deep, and I witnessed him struggle to put things into words to explain to me how he felt.

But after months of heartfelt conversations between us, I'm pleased to say that this book was a healing process for him. Soon after he believed he had shared all there was to say, we went to a traveling Vietnam Memorial wall on Father's Day. Although he couldn't bear to touch the wall, he allowed me to get rubbings for the brothers he lost. I'm happy to say that as he has healed more, he has made two trips to the wall in Washington DC, where he created the rubbings himself.

I had clung to the deployment coin of my lost love, and my father was finally given his—one from the 1st of the 502nd and one from his deployment to Vietnam—on a visit back to Fort Campbell. The significance of the coins for me is huge, and having them has been healing for both of us.

In the editorial process of this book, more memories rose to the surface and my dad was prompted to dig deeper. I won't say that didn't affect him, but I do believe it helped him to feel good that some events wouldn't be buried forever. The night his sergeant shot three of their own men has particularly haunted him. As he shared, no one was ever willing to talk about it, and so it became stuffed along with so many other disturbing events he witnessed and endured. I'm sure other veterans who read this book will reflect on similar memories, likely buried in the name of survival.

I do wonder who my father would be without Vietnam. Of course, I will never know. What I do know is that jumping from helicopters—and so much more that he was required to do as a young man who believed in his duty to help a small, war-torn country—created the man who raised me and whom I love.

Despite watching him relive this undeniably traumatic time of his life, sharing the experience of helping him bring it into book form was a privilege for which I am deeply grateful, and it has bonded us even closer than we were before.

Regardless of how you may personally feel about American involvement in the Vietnam War, whether as a veteran or a civilian, I hope you have gained an understanding of the immense sacrifices men like my father made in honorable service to their country during a very turbulent time—sacrifices that have lasted a lifetime for my dad in the form of his memories, his nightmares, his truth.

In tribute to the Men of the
1st Battalion, 502nd Airborne,
Who Were Killed in Action During My Tour

1.   Wilson, Garold SFC 30 24-Dec-67 B Co
2.   Binko, George PFC 21 27-Dec-67 A Co
3.   Cason, William PFC 21 27-Dec-67 A Co
4.   Kelman, Wayne CPL 21 04-Jan-68 C Co
5.   Long, Richard SSG 23 04-Jan-68   C Co
6.   McCray, Thomas CPL 29 04-Jan-68 C Co
7.   Roy, James SP4 20 04-Jan-68 C Co
8.   Simon, David SSG 19 04-Jan-68 C Co
9.   Sweet, Eugene PFC 18 04-Jan-68 C Co
10. Wisham, George 2LT 23 04-Jan-68 C Co
11. Gabriel, Meredith SGT 20 04-Jan-68 HHC
12. Gerwatowski, Joseph SGT 20 19-Jan-68 A Co
13. Moore, James PFC 19-Jan-68 A Co
14. Brown, John PFC 19 01-Feb-68 A Co
15. Hamilton, James SGT 19 01-Feb-68 A Co
16. Holland, Joseph CPT 25 01-Feb-68 A Co
17. Wittler, Larry PVT 19 01-Feb-68 D Co
18. Means, Ronald SP4 19 05-Feb-68 B Co
19. Brown, Raymond SP4 20 07-Feb-68 D Co
20. Urdiales, Alfred PFC 18 07-Feb-68 E Co
21. DeMello, Clyde CPL 18 09-Feb-68 A Co
22. Norton, Thomas SP4 20 09-Feb-68 A Co
23. Novel, Charles SP4 21 09-Feb-68 A Co
24. Rounseville, Joseph 1SG 30 09-Feb-68 A Co
25. Terejko, Benjamin SP4 20 09-Feb-68 A Co
26. Waite, Donald SP4 19 09-Feb-68 A Co
27. Crawford, Charles SP6 09-Feb-68 HHC
28. Saunders, Randall SP4 20 16-Feb-68 A Co
29. Vollmer, Valentine SP4 20 16-Feb-68 A Co
30. Pershing, Richard 2LT 25 17-Feb-68 A Co
31. Gregory, Henry PFC 20 17-Feb-68 B Co
32. Hoge, Frank PFC 20 17-Feb-68 B Co
33. Harrell, Ronnie PFC 19 19-Feb-68 A Co
34. Cantu, Florentino SP4 19 21-Feb-68 B Co
35. McGee, Herman PFC 21 22-Feb-68 A Co

36. Neill, Joe PFC 18 22-Feb-68 A Co
37. Zamora, Edward SP4 20 22-Feb-68 C Co
38. Combs, James SP4 19 22-Feb-68 D Co
39. Levesque, Roland SGT 21 22-Feb-68 D Co
40. Lehr, David PVT 19 23-Feb-68 D Co
41. Kromrey, Dennis PFC 21 26-Feb-68 A Co
42. Trollinger, Jimmy PFC 20 27-Feb-68 A Co
43. Borgman, Richard PFC 21 03-Mar-68 B Co
44. Fawks, Ernest SP4 30 03-Mar-68 C Co
45. Norfleet, Henry CPL 18 03-Mar-68 C Co
46. Williams, James CPL 20 03-Mar-68 C Co
47. Dimmitt, Frank CPT 30 03-Mar-68 HHC
48. Carpenter, Clinton SP4 21 06-Mar-68 D Co
49. Carr, Alvin PFC 19 06-Mar-68 D Co
50. Latraille, David SP4 20 06-Mar-68 D Co
51. Palazzola, Stephen PFC 19 06-Mar-68 D Co
52. Pigford, Phillip SGT 21 06-Mar-68 D Co
53. Shambaugh, Gregory CPL 20 06-Mar-68 D Co
54. Stys, Stanley PFC 18 06-Mar-68 D Co
55. Tedrick, Warren SGT 20 07-Mar-68 A Co
56. Arndt, Craig SP4 20 08-Mar-68 A Co
57. Bowers, William SP4 20 08-Mar-68 A Co
58. Hudson, Samuel PFC 19 08-Mar-68 A Co
59. Kidwell, Wayne SGT 19 08-Mar-68 A Co
60. Shramko, Michael PFC 19 08-Mar-68 A Co
61. Stephens, Sonnie PFC 24 08-Mar-68 A Co
62. Villafranco, Rodolfo SP4 19 08-Mar-68 A Co
63. Williams, Benharold PFC 18 08-Mar-68 A Co
64. Clewlow, Robert SGT 19 09-Mar-68 A Co
65. Hood, John SP4 18 09-Mar-68 C Co
66. Vazquez, William SP4 20 09-Mar-68 C Co
67. Kinnard, Daniel SP4 18 09-Mar-68 HHC
68. McConnell, William SP5 26 14-Mar-68 HHC
69. Blevins, Danny PFC 18 15-Mar-68 B Co
70. Jones, Benjamin SP4 20 22-Mar-68 A Co
71. Armstrong, Edwin PFC 20 26-Mar-68 B Co
72. Benn, Philip 2LT 22 26-Mar-68 B Co
73. Derrico, Jack SP4 20 26-Mar-68 B Co
74. Gibble, Alvin PFC 20 26-Mar-68 B Co
75. Horton, John PFC 21 26-Mar-68 B Co

```
 76.  Hubbard, Glen SP4 18 26-Mar-68 B Co
 77.  Krek, Philip SGT 21 26-Mar-68 B Co
 78.  Krueger, Wayne PFC 20 26-Mar-68 B Co
 79.  Link, Roger PFC 19 26-Mar-68 B Co
 80.  Smith, Joe PFC 19 26-Mar-68 B Co
 81.  Terry, Hoyle PFC 21 26-Mar-68 B Co
 82.  Barnes, John SGT 22 26-Mar-68 B Co
 83.  West, James PFC 23 31-Mar-68 A Co
 84.  Yelverton, Don SP4 18 31-Mar-68 B Co
 85.  Rhodes, Gary SGT 20 05-Apr-68 B Co
 86.  Charette, Mark SGT 19 06-Apr-68 B Co
 87.  Coughlin, Patrick PFC 19 09-Apr-68 A Co
 88.  Bell, Reginald SP4 19 16-Apr-68 D Co
 89.  Hess, Robert PFC 19 18-Apr-68 D Co
 90.  Williams, Reginald PFC 18 23-Apr-68 D Co
 91.  Alfred, Thomas PVT 18 23-Apr-68 C Co
 92.  Brown, David SP4 18 26-Apr-68 C CO
 93.  Intihar, John PFC 20 28-Apr-68 A Co
 94.  Kovaloff, Joseph SGT 20 29-Apr-68 A Co
 95.  Lutz, Larry PFC 20 30-Apr-68 A Co
 96.  Terry, Arie CPL 24 30-Apr-68 A Co
 97.  Daley, Daniel PFC 20 01-May-68 A Co
 98.  Gomez, Gelasio SSG 29 01-May-68 A Co
 99.  House, John 2LT 22 01-May-68 A Co
100. Merschel, Lawrence PFC 20 01-May-68 A Co
101. Jackson, Herman SGT 23 03-May-68 A Co
102. Brogdon, Donald CPL 18 06-May-68 A Co
103. Martinez, John SP4 20 06-May-68 A Co
104. Threet, Howard CPL 20 06-May-68 A Co
105. Hession, Patrick PFC 18 06-May-68 A Co
106. Quan, Kennth PFC 20 06-May-68 A Co
107. McLemore, Tilghman CPT 27 06-May-68 HHC
108. Clark, Jerry PFC 22 07-May-68 C Co
109. Deike, Robert PFC 20 07-May-68 C Co
110. Jeffries, Mack sGT 22 07-May-68 C Co
111. Myers, Billy SGT 21 07-May-68 C Co
112. Victor, George SFC 49  07-May-68 C Co
113. Williams, Donald CPL 24 07-May-68 C Co
114. Moran, John SGT 22 08-May-68 C Co
115. Fordi, Michael CPL 20 08-May-68 HHC
```

116. Jones, Everett SSG 28 09-May-68 D Co
117. Cooley, Shelby PFC 22 10-May-68 C Co
118. Patterson, Larry SP4 18 10-May-68 C Co
119. Luman, Ronnie SP4 21 17-May-68 C Co
120. Miller, Vernell PFC 18 27-May-68 C Co
121. Miller, Larry PFC 23 10-Jun-68 D Co
122. Collins, Toby PFC 20 11-Jun-68 E Co
123. Akin, John PFC 20 15-Jun-68 C Co
124. David, Michael SP4 24 15-Jun-68 C Co
125. Franck, Ralph PFC 20 15-Jun-68 C Co
126. Hoyt, Arthur SGT 23 15-Jun-68 C Co
127. Valenzuela, Oscar PFC 20 15-Jun-68 C Co
128. Bernard, Thomas PFC 21 16-Jun-68 B Co
129. Heiser, Edward SP4 18 28-Jun-68 D Co
130. Gregoire, Miles SGT 18 01-Jul-68 C Co
131. Weister, Ronald PFC 21 03-Jul-68 D Co
132. Templeton, Gary PFC 20 05-Jul-68 A Co
133. Hill, Randall SP4 19 13-Jul-68 A Co
134. Cox, Frank 1LT 30 14-Jul-68 A Co
135. McClafferty, James SGT 24 14-Jul-68 A Co
136. Moore, Ronnie SP4 20 18-Jul-68 C Co
137. Olenzuk, Paul PFC 22 10-Aug-68 A Co
138. Valker, George SP4 21 10-Aug-68 A Co
139. Kriskovich, Raymond SP4 24 10-Aug-68 B Co
140. Haynes, Albert PFC 20 10-Aug-68 E Co
141. Snyder, Michael SP4 21 10-Aug-68 E Co
142. Fink, Philip 1SG 41 13-Aug-68 A Co
143. Lawhorne, Donnie SP4 19 20-Aug-68 B Co
144. Gooden, Johnnie SGT 19 23-Aug-68 D Co
145. Hook, Mark PFC 18 28-Aug-68 C Co
146. Whelan, Michael SGT 20 08-Sep-68 E Co
147. Mason, James SP5 19 17-Oct-68 HHC
148. Leatutufu, Fagalii SSG 22 09-Nov-68 B Co
149. Partsafas, Terryl SP4 20 29-Nov-68 D Co
150. Weissman, Victor 1LT 21 02-Dec-68 C Co
151. Rowe, Salvatore PFC 18 13-Dec-68 B Co
152. Ludwig, James PFC 20 16-Dec-68 B Co

May my brothers rest in peace.

PHOTO
GALLERY

———

Me in my dress uniform

A family visit to Fort Leonard Wood

Me with my father, Henry

Me with my Mom, Rita, sisters Janet and Linda,
and brother Gary

Graduation after basic training, Spring 1967
Me, Gary, Mom, Janet and Linda

The famous 1960 Chevy Impala I drove to Fort
Gordon that got me into trouble
Dad and my dog Frisco are on the lawn

Me in my dress uniform. My parents had this
picture taken to put the announcement in the
paper that I was going to war.

Fort Campbell, KY, before leaving for Vietnam
The 1st of the 502nd B Company

Chopper ride

Navy pilots dropping napalm on the villages

Me with a two-poncho tent for shade

Headquarters sign at LZ Sally

Landing in a dry rice paddy
to pick up soldiers

The blown-up truck from when the smart-ass guy
saved us while we were walking

Army buddy sneaking a quick shave

Downtime and mail call with a platoon brother

The spot where we re-enacted *The Rifleman*, when I
narrowly missed Ballo
(he is standing on the porch)

Saigon, 1968

Chopper view of bombed-out areas

Me, in-country

Unknown soldier teaching the villagers how
to wash with soap. Bath time for them was in
the same water they used for toilets.

Me with the villagers, helping the South

Me, wearing my helmet that had the months written
on it, with my young village friend beside me

At a roadside tavern buying beer from the
kids. They are giggling at me because I put
on one of the girl's hats.

In-country R&R show the night I got robbed

Showing my tattoo

Washing clothes in the muddy water
on laundry day

Me with a Soviet PPSh-41 taken
from an enemy kill

A Rome plow working hard

Drying our feet and boots while
burning empty ammo crates

Guarding the engineers. Rome plow on the right,
mechanic truck on the left.

Me and a platoon buddy sitting out in the
rice paddy waiting for napalm to be dropped
on the village.

People evacuating the village to avoid napalm

Me with the 199th

Me (standing) with the 199th,
hanging out with buddies from the 101st

The photo of Rita, my then girlfriend and now
wife, that got me through the hard times.
I carry this wallet photo to this day.

ACKNOWLEDGMENTS

From John:

To my wife Rita for shielding me from the demons until I was ready to face them. And for your commitment to our marriage.

To my sons, thank you for picking up the slack around the property as I spent time on this book.

To my parents, for all your love and support for my entire life. How I wish my dad could be here to read this story.

To Carl Gordon, better known as Skippy, thank you for the daily report, which was instrumental in piecing my story together.

To Wayne Dugger, the first platoon brother to reach out to me when I started my search. You connected me with our other brothers. Thank you for fighting beside me in-country and at home.

To Ronny Ymbras, a Bravo Company brother who helped me feel less crazy when we shared our memories. Your encouragement in this venture is appreciated.

To all the members of the military, especially the 101st Airborne and the 1st of the 502nd, our brother- and sisterhood runs deep and I will always fight with you.

To my daughter Lori, thank you for telling my story and for expressing my thoughts in ways that I couldn't for fifty years.

From Lori:

To my dad, thank you for being brave to help those who so desperately sought freedom, and for finding the courage to not only share your story with me but the world too.

To my mom, for comforting and loving Dad through his struggles and for your excitement about this book, even if you will read the last page first.

To my husband Ben, thank you for nodding your head when I used you as a sounding board and for reminding me that all this was worth it when I felt discouraged.

To my dear friend Lori Hamann, thank you for not letting me quit this endeavor and for keeping me focused on the end goal.

To Stacey Aaronson, you gave this book life. So much credit needs to go to you, my biggest cheerleader who killed my inner critic.

To my motivational friend Josh Garrett, without you the rough draft would have never gotten finished so quickly, thank you.

To our advance readers who were so kind to read the book, offer positive feedback, and write heartfelt endorsements: Paul Means, Wayne Dugger, Carl Orlando, Allan Kuhlman, and Amy Shaw.

To my brothers, my best friends Cristy and Jenifer, and my fitness clients (too many to list), you have supported me and jumped with excitement over this dream. I will forever be grateful to you.

ABOUT THE BOOK

Questions for Discussion

ABOUT THE AUTHORS

A Conversation with
  John and Lori Stillman
Meet John Stillman
Meet Lori Stillman

M
O
R
E

with

J
O
H
N

and

L
O
R
I

STILLMAN

A
B
O
U
T

the

B
O
O
K

1. Were you surprised by the conditions the soldiers faced in Vietnam? If so, how did they differ from what you imagined?

2. In what ways did you witness the men finding distractions from the war? What small things seemed to have great meaning?

3. What were some of the impressions you received from John's journal entires? What struck you? Did anything surprise you?

4. At the end of Chapter 7, John laments being "worked to death" at base camp and admits he wished they were out looking for VC instead. Discuss what you made of that statement.

5. John mentions interacting with children more than once in Vietnam. What significance did you place on that interaction?

6. In Chapter 9, during gunfire in the jungle, John's buddy Waite whines about dying. In response, John states: "Of course he was going to die. We all were." At the same time, the men were made to feel indestructible. Discuss this contradiction and how you imagine it affected the soldiers.

7. In the mock standoff at the pavilion, John could have easily killed his comrade, Ballo, yet they both played it off as if they had been playing a game. How do you see this scene as a reflection of how the men came to view guns and war?

8. While hunkering down in a cemetery, John says, "At one time, it would have given me the heebie-jeebies to take refuge there, but death was different now." What do you think he meant by that?

9. How did John's mindset around killing evolve over time? What incidents do you recall that demonstrated the change?

10. How did you witness what a "good day" became for John? How did being in Vietnam shift what a "good day" meant to a solider, different from what it typically means for a civilian?

11. Could you relate to John's saying, "It was a struggle to keep myself alive. By that point, there was no way I wanted to feel responsible for anyone else." Why or why not?

12. John experienced several close calls, where his life was spared by something as negligible as a second, or a malfunctioning weapon or land mine. What impacted you in those instances? How did you relate to how he may have felt?

13. Why do you think no one was willing to talk about the incident after the sergeant killed and wounded some of his own men?

A
B
O
U
T

the

B
O
O
K

14. John described his initial homecoming "as if I wasn't really there, like it was an illusion or a dream." Putting yourself in his shoes, what do you imagine was going through his mind?

15. Why do you think John couldn't sleep in his bed after he returned home? Were you surprised he traded the comfort of it for his bedroom floor?

16. Why do you believe John found it impossible to speak about his time in Vietnam for so many years?

17. Discuss your observations of John during his homecoming party. How did you feel about the joke his father played on him?

18. Why do you think John said he would "feel like an outsider for many years to come after returning home?"

Lori, in the book's Introduction, you share that your dad had never spoken about his time in Vietnam. What was the genesis of you writing this book together?

I realized my dad had something that needed to be told and on a subject that I was desperate to know more about. Though the idea was instant, I'm still surprised today that he said yes. He then shocked me more when he told me about the journal and that my mom had his letters. It was as if the story was begging to be told, and with that, everything just fell into place.

Every book is written with a "why" behind it, and memoirs often stem from deep-seated reasons to be heard or to help others. What goal(s) did the two of you have for writing this book?

John: I mainly looked forward to spending time with Lori; I enjoyed our days talking and hanging out together. I never thought about what the end result might be.

Lori: I started out with specific goals: I wanted to heal my father, to heal my broken heart, and to heal anyone who needed it who would read the book. As my constant reminder, I actually made that mantra the background on my laptop.

ABOUT *the* AUTHORS

John, the memories you share are remarkable. Having stuffed your Vietnam experience for so long, were you surprised to find how vivid the memories still were? What did it feel like to bring it all up again after fifty years? How were you able to do so in such a linear way?

Some were not clear at first—it took four and a half years to get them into focus. I had bits and pieces that were crystal clear but were hard to bring up, especially the memories that were painful. There were times I couldn't talk because I choked on the words, so Lori would have to come back to that particular topic later. Because I didn't give the content of the book to Lori in a linear way, she had to rearrange a lot of material with me bouncing all over the timeline. But the journal, daily report, and letters to Rita helped to give her a structure, and we slowly stitched things together.

Lori, you clearly witnessed a side of your dad you hadn't previously known. How did that experience change your relationship?

I have been incredibly lucky in that I've always had a fantastic relationship with my dad. What I witnessed crushed me, and his tears definitely hurt my heart; there were times that I wondered if I was making a mistake in having him talk. But our relationship grew stronger and I now feel like I understand who he is and where his strong beliefs come from.

John, were you reluctant to open up to your daughter? Were you concerned that she would see you in a different light, or that you might feel too vulnerable doing so after years of stoicism?

No, oddly enough it felt like it was what needed to be done to tell her my story. I wasn't at all concerned that her opinion of me would change because I felt safe within our strong relationship.

Lori, your interviews with your dad must have had a deep impact on you. How did you sift through all the memories, details, and emotion to craft such a tightly woven account of your dad's time in Vietnam?

I have notebooks full of his words that I jotted down as he spoke, and I recorded all of our meetings and listened to them several times to help me. Each time we would meet, I would have questions about specific events. I also read his journal, researched things on the Internet, and kept a detailed log. All in all, I had to disconnect and play journalist to get through it.

John, did you internalize when you enlisted in the Army that you would be required to kill people, some of whom may have been innocent bystanders? How did you feel about that? Did your feelings change over time in Vietnam? Is it something that you grapple with still, or have you reconciled it somehow?

ABOUT *the* **AUTHORS**

Right out of the gate, I knew that was what my job was going to be, even when I chose infantry. I didn't have a clue what the impact of it would be, and no one said my life would never be the same. I can't say I killed anyone innocent; I don't really believe I did. But yes, my feelings changed during that time. No matter how many times I was told people would go home in a body bag, me being first, I didn't believe it would happen, because at the same time they were telling us we were indestructible. But as men were getting killed, I wrestled with that becoming my new normal. Today, I don't feel I have any problem with my actions in war because I understand I did as I was trained.

John, it's no surprise that military men were not encouraged to show emotion. As a human being embroiled in what had to be emotional situations, how do you think having to stuff that emotion affected you? Was it necessary to survive, or detrimental? Do you think the military should have a different approach to how servicemen and women are supported under these circumstances?

My generation was taught that boys don't cry, so I was raised being told not to show emotions and the military simply reinforced it. I didn't know that holding it all in would be so corrosive. Things are different today with the military—they now have more support, even though they still have a ways to go.

John, you were discharged from the Army with no debriefing, no counseling, only the question "Are you okay?" Can you share what that felt like?

The military spent ten months preparing me to go to war, yet not even ten minutes preparing me to be a civilian again. I was so messed up that all I could say was, "I'm fine." I packed it all away: the journal, the memories, my voice and my words, everything. It felt like that was what I was supposed to do. Today, I know from talking to other Vietnam veterans that those who continued on with their military career did a little better because they had other veterans to talk to. But me, I had no one who would understand.

John, you say that you were "home a long time before you were home," and that "controlling the anger took daily work." Can you share a bit more about what that was like for you, trying to assimilate into a "normal" life when you felt anything but?

To this day, I am not over this, and I'm not sure I ever will be. The only difference now is that I have tools to help me deal with it. It is a constant internal struggle to not have an outburst. Simple things can still set me off—a crowded grocery store, traffic, or even an upsetting news report.

**John, you were fortunate to find love before you
went overseas, and to have that love intact when
you returned, marrying your sweetheart. What was
Rita's role in your survival overseas? Did you and
she ever discuss your time in Vietnam after you
came home? Or was it simply part of your history
you were expected to move past?**

There were men who struggled more than I did in-
country because they received "Dear John" break-up
letters; some even committed suicide over it. I feel
like knowing that Rita was there—even just having
her picture—gave me the strength to push through.
Telling her in one of my letters that I needed her help
showed that I was counting on her. Even though she
didn't know what to do, she was there for me. To this
day, Rita and I have never talked about my time in
Vietnam.

**Lori, were there ever times for you and your
siblings growing up that your dad showed signs of
what would have been PTSD?**

Growing up, I wouldn't have known that my dad was
any different from anyone else's father. His outbursts
seemed justified to me, and I think he was always
aware that he had children around, so he tempered
his reactions. I don't personally have any memories of

him directing his anger toward us kids, but I remember my mom telling us to go play when she detected any of his anger. I do recall when my dad would work on the family car and have trouble fixing something—his frustration would come out in calling the car a "dirty whore." When I heard that, I knew to go play and leave him alone!

John, after you returned home, you finally admitted yourself to a veterans hospital for persistent rectal bleeding. Did they discover the cause? Were they able to help you recover?

They took a culture and discovered it was a strange case of parasites they had never seen before—a particular strain that they determined came from drinking water but that could have easily been in the juices of fruits (like pineapple) from being immersed in infected water. I was able to recover by taking oral medication for a year and then getting random testing throughout the years to make sure the parasites were completely killed off.

John, being a war veteran, how do you feel now when you see images of war? Are you always transported back to Vietnam? Have you had any kind of counseling to help you cope with the nightmares and disturbing images that haunt your mind?

How I may be affected depends on the image itself and how it triggers memories. I'm not always transported back to Vietnam unless the image is from

A
B
O
U
T

the

A
U
T
H
O
R
S

that time frame, but there are some things that send me back to Vietnam every single night. I have had individual counseling as well as spending two months at a PTSD center in Kansas to learn the tools to deal with the emotions. The biggest thing they suggested when I was having an episode was to tell people that I have PTSD. As weird as it sounds, as soon as I say those words out loud, I feel better. I am grateful to have something to help me now.

John, besides having spent time at the PTSD center, has anything else helped to heal you, post-Vietnam?

In the summer of 2014, my veteran's group received an invitation to attend a welcome home celebration for Vietnam veterans, which was hosted by the South Vietnamese community located in St. Louis, Missouri. That event honored both the US and South Vietnamese soldiers with a parade, music, dancing, and lots of food. I was able to share stories with Vietnamese soldiers who I possibly fought right next to in the jungles. Since that event, I have attended multiple Tet celebrations, giving it a whole new meaning for me. I've also been in attendance for events remembering the fall of Saigon, not to mention numerous picnics and lantern festivals. The reason this has helped with my healing is because I have received the most sincere thank yous from the Vietnamese community here, and I've been able to apologize for letting them down by not saving their beloved country.

Lori, having loved a military man and also now written your father's memoir with him, do you have any thoughts about how service people should be brought back into civilian life? Do you think anyone can ever truly overcome the horrors of war?

I do think things are better now than they were in 1968, but there is always room for improvement. I'd love to say that I have the perfect solution, but the truth is I don't, and the only thing I could suggest is that they spend as much time on healing our soldiers mentally as they do in training them. I would also like to see stigmas removed around mental health so that anyone struggling feels strong for reaching out instead of weak. I don't think anyone overcomes the horrors of war, but I do think they can learn to cope and function if they receive appropriate help.

John and Lori, it's clear that *Jumping from Helicopters* was a labor of love for both of you. What do you hope readers take away from this powerful story?

John: My hope is that readers get a small understanding of what combat veterans have dealt with and experienced.

Lori: I have a few things: I would like for people to have more love and less judgment, especially when dealing with someone who has experienced something traumatic. And I would like for other veterans to be encouraged to seek help and to tell their stories too.

A
B
O
U
T

the

A
U
T
H
O
R
S

Born in Chicago and raised in St. Louis, John Stillman was a quiet boy yet found fun in teasing his younger sisters and brother. His love for the Rome plows in Vietnam led him to a career as an operating engineer, where he earned a living running the big equipment on job sites. Now retired, he busies himself helping out with non-profit veterans organizations and tending to the almost one hundred acres he calls home in Missouri.

John has been happily married to his wife Rita for forty-eight years and is the father of four children, two daughters and two sons.

He still loves his road trips.

Lori Stillman started writing her story down in the form of a journal at a young age after discovering her love for books and words. Born in rural Missouri, she spent her youth exploring the forty acres of woods her parents owned, entertaining herself with a vivid imagination.

After managing a manufacturing company for twenty-two years, she reinvented herself as a certified personal trainer. Now a second-degree black belt, she loves helping people build strength and great health with her own fitness business.

A self-proclaimed tomboy and daddy's girl, Lori is a wife, fur baby momma, and travel enthusiast. Her passion for hearing people's stories sparked her interest in having her father tell his own. *Jumping from Helicopters* is her first book.

Made in the USA
Monee, IL
28 April 2021